"Information through Innovation"

A Guide to SQL
Third Edition

PHILIP J. PRATT
Grand Valley State University

boyd & fraser publishing company

Acquisitions Editor: Anne E. Hamilton
Production Editor: Jean Bermingham
Composition: Ruttle, Shaw & Wetherill, Inc.
Interior Design: Becky Herrington
Cover Design: Richard Pepper/Flying Pepper Design
Manufacturing Coordinator: Tracy Megison

© 1995 by boyd & fraser publishing company
One Corporate Place • Ferncroft Village
Danvers, Massachusetts   01923

International Thomson Publishing
boyd & fraser publishing company is an ITP company.
The ITP trademark is used under license.

Manufactured in the United States of America

Library of Congress Cataloging-in-Publication Data

Pratt, Philip J., 1945-
    A guide to SQL / Philip J. Pratt.—3rd ed.
        p.   cm.
    Includes index.
    ISBN 0-87709-520-5
    1. SQL (Computer program language)   I. Title.
QA76.73.S67P73   1994
005.75′6—dc20   94-10491
                                        CIP

1 2 3 4 5 6 7 8 9 10 M 8 7 6 5 4

CONTENTS

Structured Query Language (SQL) is becoming increasingly popular. SQL can be used by such diverse groups as home computer owners, owners of small businesses, end-users in large organizations, and programmers.

A Guide to SQL, Third Edition is intended for anyone interested in gaining familiarity with the SQL language. It is appropriate for students in introductory classes in computer science or information systems programs. It is also appropriate for anyone wishing to use SQL to access data in databases on anything from the largest mainframe to the smallest microcomputer.

This text can be used as a textbook for a stand-alone course on SQL or as a companion to a database textbook to furnish additional material on SQL. In either case, the textbook is designed to be covered from start to finish. Students should work the exercises at the ends of the chapters as they go along. The only exception to this would be in a course strictly for end-users. In such a course, instructors may not want to include the last two chapters because the material in them is rather specialized.

SPECIAL FEATURES

Use of Examples

The SQL language is presented through approximately 100 examples. Learning through examples is, for most people, the most effective way to master material.

Case Studies

A case study, the Chazy Associates database, is used throughout the examples. The same case is used in one set of exercises at the end of each chapter. Using a realistic case study makes the examples more interesting, and more real, to students. Using the same case study in a set of exercises gives a high level of continuity.

A second case study, the Movies database, is used in a second set of exercises at the end of each chapter. The second case study gives students a chance to venture out "on their own" without the direct guidance of examples from the text, thus enhancing the learning process.

Embedded Exercises

A special type of exercise, called a Q&A, is used throughout the text. These exercises are designed to be answered by students before they proceed with their reading. The intent of many of the Q&As is to make sure students understand key points in the text before they proceed. In other cases, the intent is to stimulate students to consider some special issues on their own before moving on to the presentation of these issues in the text. The answer to the Q&A is given immediately after the question. Students are encouraged to formulate their own answer before reading the one in the text. Students can thus make sure they have sufficient understanding of the material before they proceed.

Exercises   At the end of each chapter there are exercises in which students get a chance to use the features of SQL presented in the chapter to solve realistic problems. Each chapter contains two sets of exercises, one using the Chazy Associates database and one using the Movies database.

Appendix   There is a single appendix giving concise descriptions of the examples from the text. The statement of each example is included together with the SQL solution. This gives students a handy reference to the ideas covered in the text. If they want to use SQL to solve a particular problem, they can rapidly scan this index to find a similar example.

Instructor's Manual/ Transparencies   The accompanying instructor's manual contains detailed teaching tips, answers to exercises in the text, and test questions (and answers). Transparency masters are included for most of the figures in the text.

SQL2   This text includes coverage of the key features of the latest version of SQL, SQL2 (also called SQL-92).

ORGANIZATION OF THE TEXTBOOK

The textbook consists of eight chapters and an appendix.

1. Introduction   Chapter 1 introduces the concept of databases and database management systems. It also introduces the relational model as well as the two cases that are used throughout the text.

2. Data Definition   Chapter 2 covers the process of defining a database using SQL. Included in this chapter is a discussion of the role and use of nulls.

3. Single-Table Queries   Chapter 3 begins the presentation of using SQL to query a database. The queries in Chapter 3 all involve single tables. Included in this chapter are discussions of simple and compound conditions, the SQL word BETWEEN, computed columns, the SQL word LIKE, the SQL word IN, sorting, the SQL built-in functions, nesting queries, and grouping.

4. Multiple-Table Queries   Chapter 4 completes the discussion of querying a database by considering queries involving more than one table. Included in this chapter are discussions of the SQL words IN and EXISTS, subqueries within subqueries, the use of aliases, joining a table to itself, the SQL set operations, and the use of ALL and ANY.

5. Updates   Chapter 5 covers how to use SQL to update the data in a database. Included are discussions of how to change current data, add new rows, and create a new table from an existing one. In addition, the manner in which the structure of a database may be changed is examined in detail.

6. Database Administration   Chapter 6 covers the database administration features of SQL. These include views, the GRANT mechanism, indexes, and the use of the system catalog.

7. Embedded SQL   Chapter 7 covers the manner in which SQL can be embedded in a procedural language such as COBOL. Although COBOL is used as a vehicle to illustrate the concepts in this chapter, the material would apply equally well to any language that supports such an embedding. Included in this chapter are discussions of the use of embedded SQL to insert new rows, and change and delete existing rows. Also included is a discussion of how to retrieve single rows using embedded SQL and how to use cursors to retrieve multiple rows.

8. SQL2   Chapter 8 covers the important features of the latest version of SQL, SQL2.

Appendix: List of Examples   The appendix contains a concise list of all the examples presented in the text together with the associated SQL commands.

GENERAL NOTES TO THE STUDENT

Embedded Questions   At a number of places in the text, special questions have been inserted. Sometimes the purpose of these questions is to ensure that you understand some crucial material before you proceed. In other cases, the questions are designed to give you the chance to consider some special concept in advance of its actual presentation. In all cases, the answer to each question is given immediately after the question. You could simply read the question and its answer, but you will receive maximum benefit from the text if you take the time to work out the answer to the question and then check your answer against the one given in the text before you proceed with your reading.

End-of-Chapter Material   The end-of-chapter material consists of a summary and exercises. The summary briefly describes the material covered in the chapter. Scan the summary and make sure all the concepts are familiar to you. Following the summary are two sets of exercises. The first set uses the same Chazy Associates database that was used in the examples in the chapter. First work the exercises in this set to make sure you understand how the commands presented in the chapter are to be used. Then move on to the second set of exercises. The second set uses the Movies database and gives you a chance to apply what you have learned to a database that is not quite so familiar to you. (The answers to the odd-numbered exercises in both sets are given in the text.)

ACKNOWLEDGMENTS

I would like to acknowledge several individuals for their contributions in the preparation of this book.

I appreciate the efforts of the following individuals who reviewed the text and made many helpful suggestions: Ranjan B. Kini, University of North Carolina at Greensboro; Robert B. Norton, San Diego Mesa College; David Paradice, Texas A&M University; and Darleen V. Pigford, Western Kentucky University.

The efforts of the following members of the staff of boyd & fraser have been invaluable and have made this third edition possible: Tom Walker, President and Publisher; Anne Hamilton, Acquisitions Editor; Jean Bermingham, Production Editor; and Becky Herrington, Production Director.

Introduction

OBJECTIVES

When you have completed this chapter, you should understand the following:

1. The Chazy Associates database, the database that will be used in examples and exercises throughout the rest of the text.

2. The structure of a relational database.

3. The Movies database, a database that will be used in exercises throughout the text.

INTRODUCTION

A **database** is a structure that can house information about many different types of objects as well as the relationships among those objects. This text uses two databases as examples. In the Chazy Associates database, the objects are personal computers (PCs), employees, software packages, and so on. In the Movies database, which will be used in some of the exercises, the objects are directors, movies, stars, videotapes, and so on.

In addition, both databases contain information about relationships among the objects. The Chazy Associates database, for example, contains information indicating which PCs are assigned to which employees, which packages are installed on which PCs, and so forth. The Movies database has information such as which director directed which movies, which stars appeared in which movies, which movies are on which tapes, and so on.

We need a special tool to manipulate such information easily. This tool is called a **database management system** or **DBMS**. A DBMS must furnish us a method for storing and manipulating information about a variety of objects and the relationships among the objects. A DBMS is often categorized by the general approach that it takes to do this. We are interested in the general category of

1

DBMS called **relational**. We are also interested in the most popular approach for manipulating data in a relational DBMS, the language called SQL.

We begin this chapter by examining the requirements of Chazy Associates. The database for this organization will be used in the examples throughout the text, so it is important for you to become comfortable with it. Next we investigate the basic concepts of relational databases. We look at how data is structured and how data in a relational database is accessed using SQL. In the remainder of the text, we examine SQL in detail.

INTRODUCTION TO CHAZY ASSOCIATES

A large, multinational corporation, Chazy Associates needs to maintain the following information about the PCs its employees use to do their jobs.

1. For each computer, Chazy Associates needs to store the manufacturer's name and model, the processor type, and the computer ID.
2. For each employee, it needs to store the employee's number, name, and phone number.
3. For each PC, the corporation needs to store the PC's inventory tag number, computer ID, location, and the number of the employee who is the primary user of the PC.
4. For each software package, Chazy Associates needs to store the package's ID, name, version, type, and current cost.
5. For each software package installed on a PC, the corporation needs to store the software package's ID and cost, inventory tag number, and the software installation date.

Figure 1.1 represents a relational model database for Chazy Associates. Figure 1.2 shows the same database, but filled in with sample data that we will use throughout the book.

For computers, we have columns for the computer ID, manufacturer's name and model, and processor type. For employees, we have the number, name, and phone number. For PCs, we have the inventory tag number and location. In addition, we have columns in the *PC* table for computer ID and employee number. Using the computer ID in the *PC* table, we can find in the *COMPUTER* table the specific manufacturer name and model and processor type for a particular PC. Thus, we see that PC 37691 (located in Sales) has a computer ID of B121, which is a Bantam 48X 486DX. On the other hand, by looking for all the PCs that have some specific number in the *COMPID* column, we can find all similar PCs. We see then that Chazy Associates has two M759 computers (Lemmin GRL 486SX) with tag numbers 32808 (located in Accounting) and 77740 (located in the home of employee 567).

In a similar way, we can use the *EMPNUM* column in the *PC* table to find

Figure 1.1

Chazy Associates
relational database
structure

COMPUTER

COMPID	MFGNAME	MFGMODEL	PROCTYPE

EMPLOYEE

EMPNUM	EMPNAME	EMPPHONE

PC

TAGNUM	COMPID	EMPNUM	LOCATION

PACKAGE

PACKID	PACKNAME	PACKVER	PACKTYPE	PACKCOST

SOFTWARE

PACKID	TAGNUM	INSTDATE	SOFTCOST

the primary user of each PC. As examples, the primary user of PC 32808 (located in Accounting) is employee 611 (Melissa Dinh), and employee 124 (Ramon Alvarez) is the primary user of PC 37691 (located in Sales) and 59836 (located in his home).

For software packages, we have columns in the *PACKAGE* table for the ID, name, version, type, and cost. Finally, for software packages installed on Chazy Associates' PCs, we have columns in the *SOFTWARE* table for the package ID that represents the specific software package installed, the tag number that identifies the particular PC, the software package installation date, and the cost of the software package. The first row of the *SOFTWARE* table tells us, for example, that software package AC01 from Boise Accounting was installed on 09/13/95 at a cost of $754.95 on PC 32808 (located in Accounting).

To test your understanding of the relational model database for Chazy Associates, answer the following questions using the data in Figure 1.2.

Questions:

1. Give the tag numbers for all PCs that have the software package Words & More installed.
2. Give the location of the PC on which Chazy Associates has installed software

Figure 1.2

Chazy Associates
sample data

COMPUTER

COMPID	MFGNAME	MFGMODEL	PROCTYPE
B121	Bantam	48X	486DX
B221	Bantam	48D	486DX2
C007	Cody	D1	486DX
M759	Lemmin	GRL	486SX

EMPLOYEE

EMPNUM	EMPNAME	EMPPHONE
124	Alvarez, Ramon	1212
567	Feinstein, Betty	8716
611	Dinh, Melissa	2963

PC

TAGNUM	COMPID	EMPNUM	LOCATION
32808	M759	611	Accounting
37691	B121	124	Sales
57772	C007	567	Info Systems
59836	B221	124	Home
77740	M759	567	Home

PACKAGE

PACKID	PACKNAME	PACKVER	PACKTYPE	PACKCOST
AC01	Boise Accounting	3.00	Accounting	725.83
DB32	Manta	1.50	Database	380.00
DB33	Manta	2.10	Database	430.18
SS11	Limitless View	5.30	Spreadsheet	217.95
WP08	Words & More	2.00	Word Processing	185.00
WP09	Freeware Processing	4.27	Word Processing	30.00

SOFTWARE

PACKID	TAGNUM	INSTDATE	SOFTCOST
AC01	32808	09/13/95	754.95
DB32	32808	12/03/95	380.00
DB32	37691	06/15/95	380.00
DB33	57772	05/27/95	412.77
WP08	32808	01/12/96	185.00
WP08	37691	06/15/95	227.50
WP08	57772	05/27/95	170.24
WP09	59836	10/30/95	35.00
WP09	77740	05/27/95	35.00

package AC01. Give the name of the employee who is the primary user of this PC.

3. List all the software packages installed on PC tag number 57772. For each package, give the installation date, name, version, and type.
4. Why is the column *SOFTCOST* part of the *SOFTWARE* table? Can't we just take the *PACKID* and look up the cost in the *PACKAGE* table?

Answers:

1. 32808, 37691, and 57772. (Look up the package ID of Words & More in the *PACKAGE* table and obtain WP08. Then find all tag numbers in the *SOFTWARE* table that have WP08 in the *PACKID* column.)
2. Accounting. Melissa Dinh. (Look up package ID AC01 in the *SOFTWARE* table and obtain tag number 32808. Then find the row in the *PC* table that has tag number 32808 and obtain a location of Accounting. Using this same row's employee number of 611, find the name of the employee in the *EMPLOYEE* table.)
3. 05/27/95, Manta, 2.10, Database. 05/27/92, Words & More, 2.00, Word Processing. (Look up each *SOFTWARE* table row in which the tag number is 57772. Each row contains an installation date. Use the package ID to look up the corresponding name, version, and type in the *PACKAGE* table.)
4. If we don't have the *SOFTCOST* column in the *SOFTWARE* table, we must obtain the cost for an installed package by looking up *PACKCOST* in the *PACKAGE* table. *PACKCOST* represents the current package cost, which is not necessarily the cost of the package when it was installed because vendors can raise or lower the prices they charge at any time. Thus, we include the *SOFTCOST* column in the *SOFTWARE* table so we can retain the actual package cost at the time of installation. (**Note:** If you examine the *SOFTWARE* table, you will see cases in which the *SOFTCOST* value matches the current price in the *PACKAGE* table and cases in which it differs.)

INTRODUCTION TO THE RELATIONAL DATABASES

Structure

You have already seen a relational database. A relational database is just a collection of tables like the ones for Chazy Associates in Figure 1.2. You might wonder why such a database is not called a "table" database or something similar, if a database is a collection of tables. Formally, these tables are called **relations,** the source of this name's approach.

How does such a DBMS handle objects and the relationships among these objects? Handling the objects is fairly simple. Each object gets a table of its own. Thus, in the database for Chazy Associates, there is a table for employees, a separate table for PCs, and so on. The important properties of the objects become the columns in the table. In the table for employees, for example, there is a column for the employee number, a column for the employee name, and so on.

What about relationships? At Chazy Associates, there is a one-to-many relationship between employees and PCs (each employee is related to the many PCs he or she is assigned, and each PC is related to the one employee to whom the PC is assigned). How is this relationship implemented in a relational database? The answer is, through common columns in two or more tables. Consider Figure 1.2 again. The column *EMPNUM* of the employee table and the column *EMPNUM* of the PC table are used to implement the relationship between employees and

PCs; that is, given an employee, we can use these columns to determine all the PCs he or she is assigned, and, given a PC, we can use these columns to find the employee to whom the PC is assigned.

Let us now refine our description of a relation. A relation is a two-dimensional table. If we consider the tables in Figure 1.2, however, we can see that there are certain restrictions we would probably want to place on relations. Each column should have a unique name, and entries within each column should all "match" this column name; that is, if the column name is *EMPNAME*, all entries in that column should in fact be employee names. Also, each row should be unique. If two rows are absolutely identical, after all, the second row doesn't give us any information we don't already have. In addition, for maximum flexibility, the ordering of the columns and the rows should be immaterial. Finally, the table will be simplest if each position is restricted to a single entry: that is, if we do not allow multiple entries (often called **repeating groups**) in an individual location in the table. In summary, a relation is a two-dimensional table with the following characteristics:

1. The entries in the table are single-valued (that is, each location in the table contains a single entry).
2. Each column has a distinct name (technically, the attribute name).
3. All the values in a column are values of the same attribute (that is, all entries must match the column name).
4. The order of columns is immaterial.
5. Each row is distinct.
6. The order of rows is immaterial.

A **relational database** is simply a collection of relations. Each row of a relation is technically called a **tuple**, and each column is formally called an **attribute**. Thus, we have two different sets of terms: relation, tuple, attribute; and table, row, and column. There is even a third set. The table could be viewed as a file (in fact, this is how relational databases are often stored, with each relation in a separate file). In this case, we would call the rows records and the columns fields. We now have *three* different sets of terms! Their correspondence is shown below:

Formal Terms	Alternative 1	Alternative 2
relation	table	file
tuple	row	record
attribute	column	field

Of these three sets of choices, the one that is becoming the most popular is alternative 1: table, row, and column. One reason for its popularity is that it seems the most natural to the nontechnical user. A second reason is that many (if not most) of the commercial relational DBMSs use this set of terms. All the terms are often used interchangeably. In this text, we will use the terms *table*, *row*, and *column*.

It would be nice to have a concise way of indicating the tables and columns in a relational database without having to draw the tables themselves, as we did in Figure 1.2. Perhaps we could draw some empty tables, such as those in Figure 1.1, but this seems rather cumbersome. Fortunately, there is a commonly accepted shorthand representation of the structure of a relational database. We merely write the name of the table and then, within parentheses, list all the columns in the table. Thus, this sample database consists of:

```
COMPUTER (COMPID, MFGNAME, MFGMODEL, PROCTYPE)

EMPLOYEE (EMPNUM, EMPNAME, EMPPHONE)

PC (TAGNUM, COMPID, EMPNUM, LOCATION)

PACKAGE (PACKID, PACKNAME, PACKVER, PACKTYPE, PACKCOST)

SOFTWARE (PACKID, TAGNUM, INSTDATE, SOFTCOST)
```

Notice that there is some duplication of names. The column *COMPID* appears in both the *COMPUTER* table and the *PC* table, which could be confusing. If we merely wrote *COMPID*, how would the computer know which *COMPID* we meant? For that matter, how would a person looking at what we had written know which one we meant? We need a mechanism for indicating the column to which we are referring. One common approach to this problem is to write both the table name and the column name, separated by a period. Thus, the *COMPID* in the *PC* table would be written *PC.COMPID*, whereas the *COMPID* in the *COMPUTER* table would be written *COMPUTER.COMPID*. Technically, when we do this, we say that we **qualify** the names. It is always acceptable to qualify data names, even if there is no possibility of confusion. If confusion may arise, however, it is *essential* to do so.

There is one other important topic to discuss before we leave the structure part of relational databases. The **primary key** of a table (relation) is the column or collection of columns that uniquely identifies a given row. In the *COMPUTER* table, for example, the employee's number uniquely identifies a given row. For instance, employee 6 occurs in only one row of the table. Thus, *COMPID* is the primary key. Primary keys are typically indicated in the shorthand representation by underlining the column or collection of columns that comprises the primary key. Thus, the complete shorthand representation for the Chazy Associates database would be:

```
COMPUTER (COMPID, MFGNAME, MFGMODEL, PROCTYPE)

EMPLOYEE (EMPNUM, EMPNAME, EMPPHONE)

PC (TAGNUM, COMPID, EMPNUM, LOCATION)

PACKAGE (PACKID, PACKNAME, PACKVER, PACKTYPE, PACKCOST)

SOFTWARE (PACKID, TAGNUM, INSTDATE, SOFTCOST)
```

Q & A

Question: Why does the primary key to the *SOFTWARE* table consist of two columns, not just one?

Answer: No single column in this table uniquely identifies a given row. It requires two columns: *PACKID* and *TAGNUM*.

Operations (Introduction to SQL)

To make a database useful, we need to be able to add data to it, change the data currently in it, and delete data from it. We also need to be able to query the database, that is, ask questions. For example, we may want to find out which customers have a balance that exceeds their credit limit. We want to produce reports, such as a listing of information about all parts. A DBMS must furnish the necessary operations so that we can accomplish such tasks.

A DBMS can take many different approaches to do this. The approach that is becoming the most prevalent is the language called **SQL (Structured Query Language)**. The language was originally developed by IBM in the 1970s as part of a prototype relational model DBMS called System R. It is also the foundation for two commercial DBMSs IBM released in the 1980s, SQL/DS and DB2. Many other relational DBMSs either currently use SQL or plan to use it in the future. Standards for SQL were approved by the American National Standards Institute (ANSI) in 1986. If you will be working with databases in any capacity, it is very likely that you will use SQL for at least some of your work. Thus, this is a very important language for you to learn.

The basic form of an SQL command (also called an SQL query) is simply

```
SELECT ... <columns>
    FROM ... <tables>
    WHERE ... <restrictions>
```

The above notation indicates that we list the columns that we wish to see printed after the word SELECT. After the word FROM, we list all tables that contain these columns. Finally, we list any restrictions to be applied after the word WHERE. We will be looking at this language in detail throughout the text. For now, however, let's look at two brief examples. First, suppose we want to print the name of the employee whose number is 124. We want to print the employee name (the column is called *EMPNAME*) from the employee table (the table is called *EMPLOYEE*) for the row on which the customer number (the column is called *EMPNUM*) is equal to 124. The appropriate SQL command is thus:

```
SELECT EMPNAME
     FROM EMPLOYEE
     WHERE EMPNUM = 124
```

The computer responds with:

```
EMPNAME
Alvarez, Ramon
```

If we wanted to find the number and name of the employee whose phone is 2963, we would type:

```
SELECT EMPNUM, EMPNAME
     FROM EMPLOYEE
     WHERE EMPPHONE = 2963
```

and the computer would respond with:

```
EMPNUM EMPNAME
   567 Feinstein, Betty
```

THE MOVIES DATABASE

While the Chazy Associates database will be used for examples in the text and also in many of the exercises, there is another database, involving movies, that will be used for another set of exercises.

As a hobby, Lee gathers and organizes facts on movies, directors, and movie stars. When she adds a new movie to her files, she assigns it a number that she uses for reference purposes. In addition to this number, she keeps the title of the movie; the type of movie; the year it was produced; the critics' rating (number of stars awarded); the rating of the MPAA (Motion Picture Association of America); the number of Academy Award nominations it received; and the number of Academy Awards it won.

Similarly, she assigns a number to the directors she adds to the files. She also keeps the director's name, the year in which he or she was born, and, if appropriate, the year in which he or she died. Actors and actresses are likewise assigned numbers when they are added to the files. Also filed are the star's name, birthplace, the year born, and, again, if appropriate, the year died.

Lee wants to use this information in a variety of ways, such as the following:

1. For each director, list his or her number, name, the year in which he or she was born, and (if deceased) the year of death.
2. For each movie, list its number, title, the year in which it was made, and its type.
3. For each movie, list its number, title, the number and name of its director, the critics' rating, the MPAA rating, the number of awards the movie was nominated for, and the number it won.
4. For each movie star, list his or her number, name, birthplace, the year in which he or she was born, and (if deceased) the year of death.
5. For each movie, list its number and title, along with the number and name of all the stars who appeared in it.
6. For each movie star, list his or her number and name, along with the number and name of all the movies in which he or she starred.

Lee has determined that the best way to manage this data is to use a relational DBMS. Accordingly, she has decided how to organize the data into tables. The first of Lee's tables is the one shown in Figure 1.3. It is called *DIRECTOR* and contains information on movie directors. Each director's record contains the number that Lee has arbitrarily assigned to him or her, his or her name, the year in which the director was born, and, if appropriate, the year in which he or she died. (In this and other figures, the symbol "-" indicates that there is no value in that position in the table. In this case, it signifies that the director is still living.)

Figure 1.3

DIRECTOR table

DIRECTOR

DIRNUMB	DIRNAME	DIRBORN	DIRDIED
1	Allen, Woody	1935	-
2	Hitchcock, Alfred	1899	1980
3	De Mille, Cecil B.	1881	1959
4	Kramer, Stanley	1913	-
5	Kubrick, Stanley	1928	-
6	Preminger, Otto	1906	-
7	Ford, John	1895	1973

Lee uses numbers for directors because it is usually simpler to refer to the directors that way. If she happens to forget a director's number, she can easily enter the director's name and quickly find the number.

In a table called *STAR* (see Figure 1.4), Lee keeps information on actors and actresses. Each row in this table contains the star's number, name, birthplace, the year in which the star was born, and, again, if appropriate, the year in which he or she died.

Another table in Lee's system is called *MOVIE* (see Figure 1.5). For each

Figure 1.4

STAR table

STAR

STARNUMB	STARNAME	BRTHPLCE	STARBORN	STARDIED
1	Allen, Woody	New York	1935	–
2	Keaton, Diane	Los Angeles	1946	–
3	Sellers, Peter	Southsea, Eng.	1925	1980
4	Scott, George C.	Wise, Va.	1927	–
5	McDowell, Malcolm	Leeds, Eng.	1943	–
6	Grant, Cary	Bristol, Eng.	1904	1986
7	Saint, Eva Marie	Newark, N.J.	1929	–
8	Stewart, James	Indiana, Pa.	1908	–
9	Perkins, Anthony	New York	1932	–
10	Leigh, Janet	Merced, Cal.	1927	–
11	Taylor, Rod	Sydney, Australia	1930	–
12	Hedren, Tippi	Lafayette, Minn.	1935	–
13	Mature, Victor	Louisville, Ky.	1916	–
14	Tracy, Spencer	Milwaukee	1900	1967
15	Hepburn, Katharine	Hartford	1909	–
16	Dullea, Keir	Cleveland	1939	–
17	Novak, Kim	Chicago	1933	–
18	Sinatra, Frank	Hoboken, N.J.	1915	–
19	March, Fredric	Racine, Wis.	1897	1975
20	Andrews, Dana	Collins, Miss.	1912	–
21	Heston, Charlton	Evanston, Ill.	1923	–
22	McNamara, Maggie	New York	1928	1978
23	Niven, David	Kirriemuir, Scot.	1910	1983
24	Wayne, John	Winterset, Iowa	1907	1979
25	Gable, Clark	Cadiz, O.	1901	1960
26	Kelly, Grace	Philadelphia	1929	1982
27	Fonda, Henry	Grand Island, Neb.	1905	1982

movie, the table contains a number, the title, the year in which the movie was produced, the type of movie (comedy, drama, science fiction, and so on), the critics' rating, the MPAA rating, the number of Academy Award nominations the movie received, the number of Academy Awards it won, and the number of the director.

The table called *MOVSTAR*, shown in Figure 1.6, is used simply to relate actors and actresses to the movies in which they appeared.

Question: To check your understanding of how Lee implemented relationships between directors and movies, answer the following questions: Who directed the movie *Dr. Strangelove*? Which movies listed in Figure 1.5 did Woody Allen direct?

Answer: The director number (*DIRNUMB*) in the row in the *MOVIE* table in which *MVTITLE* is *Dr. Strangelove* is 5. Examining the *DIRECTOR* table, we see that 5 is the number assigned to Stanley Kubrick.

To find the movies directed by Woody Allen, we look up his number in the

MOVIE

MVNUMB	MVTITLE	YRMDE	MVTYPE	CRIT	MPAA	NOMS	AWRD	DIRNUMB
1	Annie Hall	1977	COMEDY	4	PG	5	4	1
2	Dr. Strangelove	1964	COMEDY	4	PG	4	0	5
3	Clockwork Orange	1971	SCI FI	4	R	3	0	5
4	North by Northwest	1959	SUSPEN	4	PG	1	0	2
5	Rope	1948	SUSPEN	3	NR	0	0	2
6	Psycho	1960	HORROR	4	PG	3	0	2
7	Interiors	1978	DRAMA	3	PG	3	0	1
8	The Birds	1963	HORROR	3	NR	0	0	2
9	Samson and Delilah	1949	RELIGI	2	NR	1	0	3
10	Guess Who's Coming to Dinner	1967	COMEDY	3	NR	6	2	4
11	Manhattan	1979	COMEDY	4	R	2	0	1
12	Vertigo	1958	SUSPEN	4	NR	0	0	2
13	Judgment at Nuremberg	1961	DRAMA	3	NR	6	2	4
14	2001	1968	SCI FI	4	G	2	0	5
15	The Man with the Golden Arm	1955	DRAMA	3	NR	1	0	6
16	Anatomy of a Murder	1959	SUSPEN	4	NR	4	0	6
17	Inherit the Wind	1960	DRAMA	4	NR	2	0	4
18	Laura	1944	SUSPEN	4	NR	3	1	6
19	The Ten Commandments	1956	RELIGI	3	NR	1	0	3
20	The Moon Is Blue	1953	COMEDY	2	NR	1	0	6
21	Stagecoach	1939	WESTER	4	NR	3	1	7
22	Rear Window	1954	SUSPEN	4	NR	1	0	2
23	Mogambo	1953	WESTER	3	NR	2	0	7
24	Grapes of Wrath	1940	DRAMA	4	NR	4	2	7

Figure 1.5

MOVIE table

DIRECTOR table and see that it is 1. Next, we look for all records in the *MOVIE* table for which the director number is 1 and find that Woody Allen directed *Annie Hall*, *Interiors*, and *Manhattan*.

Question: To check your understanding of how Lee implemented relationships between movies and stars, answer the following questions: Who starred in *Dr. Strangelove*? Which of the movies listed in Figure 1.5 starred James Stewart?

Answer: To determine who starred in *Dr. Strangelove*, we first examine the *MOVIE* table to find its movie number (2). Next we look for all rows in the *MOVSTAR* table in which the movie number (*MVNUMB*) is 2. There are two such rows. In one of them, the star number (*STARNUMB*) is 3, and in the other, it is 4. All that is left is to look in the *STAR* table to find the actors or actresses who have been assigned the numbers 3 and 4. The answer is Peter Sellers and George C. Scott.

To find the movies that starred James Stewart, we look up his number in the

Figure 1.6

MOVSTAR table

MOVSTAR

MVNUMB	STARNUMB
1	1
1	2
2	3
2	4
3	5
4	6
4	7
5	8
6	9
6	10
7	2
8	11
8	12
9	13
10	14
10	15
11	1
11	2
12	8
12	17
13	14
14	16
15	17
15	18
16	8
17	14
17	19
18	20
19	21
20	22
20	23
21	24
22	8
22	26
23	25
23	26
24	27

STAR table and find that it is 8. Then we look for all rows in the *MOVSTAR* table for which the star number is 8. There are four such rows. The corresponding movie numbers are 5, 12, 16, and 22. Looking up these numbers in the *MOVIE* table, we find that James Stewart starred in *Rope*, *Vertigo*, *Anatomy of a Murder*, and *Rear Window*.

Lee has recently started a video rental store that she calls Lee's Video Club. She refers to each of her customers as "members." Each member in the club is assigned a number. She also keeps the members' names and addresses. In addition, she stores the number of rentals the member has made, the number of bonus units the member is currently qualified for, and the date the member joined the club. (Lee periodically has promotions during which members can earn bonus units, which they can later apply to the cost of renting tapes.) She keeps this information in a table called *MEMBER* (see Figure 1.7).

Figure 1.7

MEMBER table

MEMBER

MMBNUMB	MMBNAME	MMBADDR	MMBCTY	MMBST	NUMRENT	BONUS	JOINDATE
1	Allen, Donna	21 Wilson	Carson	In	2	0	05/25/95
2	Peterson, Mark	215 Raymond	Cedar	In	14	1	02/20/94
3	Sanchez, Miguel	47 Chipwood	Mantin	Il	22	0	06/14/94
4	Tran, Thanh	108 College	Carson	In	3	0	07/03/95
5	Roberts, Terry	602 Bridge	Hudson	Mi	1	0	11/16/94
6	MacDonald, Greg	19 Oak	Carson	In	11	1	01/29/95
7	VanderJagt, Neal	12 Bishop	Mantin	Il	19	2	08/11/94
8	Shippers, John	208 Grayton	Cedar	In	6	1	09/02/95
9	Franklin, Trudy	103 Bedford	Brook	Mi	27	3	12/13/94
10	Stein, Shelly	82 Harcourt	Hudson	Mi	4	0	06/21/95

Finally, Lee keeps information on the videotapes the club owns. When the club purchases a videotape, she assigns it a number. Along with the number, Lee stores the number of the movie on the tape, the date the tape was purchased, the number of times the tape has been rented, and the number of the member who is currently renting the tape. (If the tape is not currently being rented, the member number will appear as "-".) She keeps this information in a table called *TAPE* (see Figure 1.8).

Question: Again, to check your understanding of the meaning of the data in these tables, answer the following questions: Which members are currently renting movies? For each tape that is currently rented, give the tape number, the number and name of the member who has rented the tape, the title of the movie, the name of the director, and the names of all the stars who appeared in the movie.

Answer: To determine the members who are currently renting tapes, look at the *MMBNUMB* column in the *TAPE* table for those entries that are not "-". You will obtain the numbers 2, 3, 4, 6, 7, 8, and 10. Look up these numbers in the *MMBNUMB* column of the *MEMBER* table, and you will find the members who currently have tapes are Mark Peterson, Miguel Sanchez, Thanh Tran, Greg Mac-Donald, Neal VanderJagt, John Shippers, and Shelly Stein.

The tapes that are currently rented are represented by those rows in the *TAPE* table that do not have "-" in the *MMBNUMB* column. For each of these rows, use

Figure 1.8

TAPE table

TAPE

TPNUMB	MVNUMB	PURDATE	TMSRNT	MMBNUMB
1	1	04/26/94	4	-
2	2	04/26/94	2	2
3	3	04/26/94	6	-
4	4	04/28/94	8	10
5	5	05/12/94	3	4
6	6	05/12/94	8	-
7	7	05/12/94	2	2
8	8	05/12/94	9	8
9	6	06/26/94	1	-
10	9	06/26/94	7	3
11	10	06/26/94	10	-
12	11	07/11/94	6	6
13	12	08/02/94	4	-
14	6	08/02/94	5	-
15	13	08/25/94	2	2
16	14	08/25/94	7	-
17	15	09/07/94	11	-
18	16	09/07/94	6	8
19	17	09/23/94	3	-
20	14	10/12/94	4	3
21	18	11/15/94	8	-
22	19	11/15/94	3	-
23	20	12/21/94	4	-
24	21	01/11/95	9	7
25	22	02/14/95	2	-
26	23	02/14/95	1	-
27	24	03/06/95	4	3

the value in the *MVNUMB* column and look up the movie in the *MOVIE* table for which the *MVNUMB* column is the same. Once you have found the movie, you can find the remaining information in the same manner as before. In the second row of the *TAPE* table, for example, *MVNUMB* is 2, so the movie is *Dr. Strangelove*, the director is Stanley Kubrick, and the stars are Peter Sellers and George C. Scott.

The shorthand representation for this database is as follows:

```
DIRECTOR (DIRNUMB, DIRNAME, DIRBORN, DIRDIED)

STAR (STARNUMB, STARNAME, BRTHPLCE, STARBORN, STARDIED)

MOVIE (MVNUMB, MVTITLE, YRMDE, MVTYPE, CRIT, MPAA, NOMS,
       AWRD, DIRNUMB)

MOVSTAR (MVNUMB, STARNUMB)
```

```
MEMBER (MMBNUMB, MMBNAME, MMBADDR, MMBCTY, MMBST, NUMRENT,
        BONUS, JOINDATE)

TAPE (TPNUMB, MVNUMB, PURDATE, TMSRNT, MMBNUMB)
```

SUMMARY

Following is a summary of the material covered in Chapter 1:

1. A database is a structure that can house information about many different types of objects and about the relationships between these objects.
2. A database management system (DBMS) is a software package whose function is to manipulate a database as directed by users.
3. Chazy Associates is an organization whose requirements include the following objects:
    a. computers
    b. employees
    c. PCs
    d. software packages
    e. records of installed software
4. A relation is a two-dimensional table in which
    a. the entries are single-valued;
    b. each column has a distinct name;
    c. all the values in a column are values of the same attribute (the one identified by the column name);
    d. the order of columns is immaterial;
    e. each row is distinct; and
    f. the order of rows is immaterial.
5. A relational database is a collection of relations.
6. The terms *relation, tuple,* and *attribute* correspond to the terms *table, row,* and *column,* respectively.
7. The terms *relation, tuple,* and *attribute* also correspond to the terms *file, record,* and *field,* respectively.
8. The primary key is the column or columns that uniquely identify a given row within the table.
9. SQL is a language used to manipulate relational databases. The basic form of an SQL command is SELECT-FROM-WHERE.
10. A column name is qualified by preceding it with the table name and a period, for example, *COMPUTER.COMPID.*
11. The Movies database contains information about the following objects:
    a. directors
    b. stars
    c. movies
    d. tapes
    e. members

EXERCISES (CHAZY ASSOCIATES)

Answer each of the following questions using the Chazy Associates data as shown in Figure 1.2. No computer work is involved. In later chapters, you will find the answers to questions using SQL.

1. Find the model names of all computers with a 486DX processor.
2. Give the tag numbers of those PCs assigned to employee 124 and whose location is "Home."
3. List the computer ID and model name for those computers with a 486DX or a 486DX2 processor.
4. List the tag numbers and computer IDs for those PCs whose location is not "Home."
5. List the package IDs and names of all packages whose cost is between $200 and $500 (not including $200 or $500).
6. Give the package ID, name, version, and discounted package cost (package cost times .90) for each package whose type is Database.
7. Give the package ID, name, version, and discounted package cost for each package whose discounted cost is at least $400.
8. List the package IDs and names of all parts whose type is Database or Spreadsheet.
9. Find the numbers and names of any employee whose last name is Feinstein.
10. List all details about packages. Sort the output by package name.
11. List all details about packages. Sort the output by descending package type within package type.
12. Find out how many packages cost more than $400.00.
13. Find the average package cost for packages whose type is Word Processing.
14. List the package ID and name for all packages whose cost is above average.
15. List the average package cost for packages of each type. Then list only the averages for types containing more than one package.
16. For each PC, list the tag number and computer ID along with the name of the computer manufacturer.
17. For each PC assigned to employee 124, list the tag number and computer ID along with the name of the computer manufacturer.
18. For each PC, list the tag number and computer ID. In addition, for each software package installed on the PC, list the package ID, the package name, and the date of installation.
19. Find the numbers and names of all employees who are assigned a PC for home use (that is, the location is "Home").
20. Find the numbers and names of all employees who are not assigned a PC for home use.
21. For each PC, list the tag number and computer ID, as well as the name, version, and type of all packages installed on the PC.
22. Find the manufacturer names and models of all PCs that are assigned to at least one employee who uses the computer at home.

23. Find the tag number and computer IDs for those PCs that have at least one Database package installed on them.
24. List the package IDs and names of pairs of packages that are of the same type.
25. List the tag numbers and computer IDs of any PCs assigned to Ramon Alvarez (Alvarez, Ramon) that have a database package installed on them.
26. List the tag numbers and computer IDs of any PCs assigned to Ramon Alvarez that do not have a database package installed on them.
27. List the tag numbers and computer IDs of any PCs assigned to Ramon Alvarez or that have a database package installed on them.
28. List the package ID and name for all packages that have a package cost greater than the package cost of any package whose type is Database.

EXERCISES (MOVIES)

Answer each of the following questions using the Movies data as shown in Figures 1.3 through 1.8. No computer work is involved. In later chapters, you will find the answers to questions using SQL.

1. List the numbers, names, and addresses of all members.
2. List the numbers and titles of all movies.
3. List the complete *DIRECTOR* table.
4. List the names of all directors born during or after 1920.
5. List the tape numbers of all tapes that have been rented at least 10 times.
6. List the numbers and titles of all movies that have won at least one Academy Award.
7. List the numbers and titles of all movies whose MPAA rating is PG.
8. List the numbers and titles of all movies whose MPAA rating is PG and that were nominated for at least one Academy Award.
9. List the numbers and titles of all movies that were rated PG or that won at least one Academy Award.
10. List the numbers and titles of all movies that have an MPAA rating. (If a movie does not have an MPAA rating, its rating is listed as NR, which stands for "not rated.")
11. List the member numbers and names of all members who have rented between 10 and 20 tapes.
12. List the numbers and names of all directors who are still living.
13. List the numbers, names, and ages (year died minus year of birth) of all movie stars who are deceased.
14. Find the numbers and names of all directors whose first name is Stanley.
15. List the numbers and titles of all movies whose type is COMEDY, RELIGI, or SUSPEN.
16. List the numbers, names, addresses, and join dates of all members. Sort the output by name.

17. List the numbers, names, addresses, and join dates of all members. Sort the output by city within state.
18. List the numbers, names, addresses, and join dates of all members. Sort the output by join date. List the most recent member first.
19. Find out how many movies are of type SUSPEN.
20. Find out how many movies are of type SUSPEN, the total number of awards for which these movies were nominated, and the total number of awards they won.
21. Count the number of members who are currently renting tapes.
22. Find the maximum number of awards that any movie directed by director 5 was nominated for. Find *all* movies (any director) that won at least as many awards as this maximum.
23. List the numbers and names of all members who have rented more tapes than average.
24. For each director, find the total number of awards won by movies he or she has directed.
25. Repeat Exercise 24, but only list the directors for whom the total number of awards is at least 4.
26. For each director, find the total number of awards won by comedies (movies whose type is COMEDY) he or she has directed.
27. Repeat Exercise 26, but only list the directors for whom the total number of awards is at least 1.
28. For each movie, list the movie number, title, and number and name of the director.
29. For each tape, list the tape number and purchase date along with the number and title of the movie on the tape.
30. For each movie of type COMEDY, list the movie number and title along with the number and name of the director of the movie.
31. For each tape that has been rented at least five times, list the tape number and purchase date along with the number and title of the movie on the tape.
32. For each tape that is currently rented, list the tape number and the movie number as well as the number and name of the member who is currently renting the tape.
33. Find the numbers and names of all directors who have directed at least one comedy.
34. Find the numbers and names of all directors who have never directed a comedy (at least, as far as the data in this database indicates).
35. For each movie, list the title of the movie, together with the names and birthplaces of all the stars who appeared in the movie.
36. List the numbers and names of all stars in the database who have appeared in at least one comedy.
37. List the numbers and names of all stars who have appeared in any movies directed by Alfred Hitchcock.
38. List the numbers and names of any pairs of movies that are of the same type and have the same director.

39. For each movie, list the title, the name of the director, and the names of all the stars who appeared in the movie.
40. List the tape numbers and movie numbers for all tapes on which the movie is a comedy and that are currently rented by Mark Peterson.
41. List the tape numbers and movie numbers for all tapes on which the movie is a comedy or that are rented by Mark Peterson.
42. List the tape numbers and movie numbers for all tapes on which the movie is a comedy but that are currently rented by someone other than Mark Peterson.
43. List the movie numbers and titles for all movies that were nominated for more Academy Awards than any movies directed by Woody Allen.

Data Definition

OBJECTIVES

When you have completed this chapter, you should understand the following:

1. How to create tables using SQL.
2. The possible data types that can be used in SQL tables.
3. The meaning and use of nulls.
4. How to load data into a database.

INTRODUCTION

In this chapter we investigate the manner in which databases are initially created. This entails describing all the tables and columns that make up the database to SQL. We discuss the possible data types that can be used in this process. We also explain a special type of value called a null value and see how such values are handled during database creation. Finally, we investigate how to load a database. Loading a database simply means adding the initial data to the newly created tables.

DATABASE CREATION

Database Description

We must describe the layout of each table in the database before we can begin loading and accessing data.

Example 1: Describe the layout of the package table to the DBMS.

The SQL statement used to describe the layout of a table is CREATE TABLE. The word TABLE is followed by the name of the table to be created and then by the names and data types of the columns that comprise the table. The rules for naming tables and columns vary slightly from one version of SQL to another. If you have any doubts about the validity of any of the names you have chosen, you should consult a manual on the subject. Typical restrictions are:

1. The name can be no longer than 18 characters.
2. The name must start with a letter.
3. The name can contain letters, numbers, and underscores (__).
4. The name cannot contain spaces.

The names used in this text should work on any SQL implementation.

In Example 1, the appropriate statement is:

```
CREATE TABLE PACKAGE
    (PACKID          CHAR(4),
     PACKNAME        CHAR(20),
     PACKVER         DECIMAL(3,2),
     PACKTYPE        CHAR(15),
     PACKCOST        DECIMAL(5,2))
```

In this SQL statement, which uses the data definition features of SQL, we're describing a table that will be called *PACKAGE*. It contains five columns: *PACKID*, *PACKNAME*, *PACKVER*, *PACKTYPE*, and *PACKCOST*. *PACKID* is a 4-character alphanumeric field. *PACKNAME* is a 20-character alphanumeric field and *PACK-TYPE* is a 15-character alphanumeric field. *PACKVER* is numeric and is 3 digits long, including 2 decimal places. Similarly, *PACKCOST* is 5 digits long, and 2 of those are decimal places. We can visualize this statement as setting up for us a blank table with appropriate column headings (see Figure 2.1).

Figure 2.1

Blank PACKAGE table

PACKAGE

PACKID	PACKNAME	PACKVER	PACKTYPE	PACKCOST

Note: In SQL, commands are free-format. No rule says that a particular word must begin in a particular position on the line. The previous SQL command could have been written:

```
CREATE TABLE PACKAGE (PACKID CHAR(4), PACKNAME CHAR(20), PACKVER
DECIMAL(3,2), PACKTYPE CHAR(15), PACKCOST DECIMAL(5,2))
```

The manner in which it was actually written simply makes the command more readable. Throughout the text, we will strive for such readability when we write SQL commands.

Data Types   Besides the data types DECIMAL (numeric) and CHAR (text), there are others. While the actual data types will vary somewhat from one implementation of SQL to another, the following list indicates the common types:

1. **INTEGER.** Integers, or numbers without a decimal part. Range is −2147483648 to 2147483647.
2. **SMALLINT.** Like INTEGER but does not occupy as much space. Range is −32768 to 32767. This is a better choice than INTEGER if you are certain that numbers will be in the indicated range.
3. **DECIMAL (p,q).** Decimal number p digits long, with q of these being decimal places. For example, DECIMAL (5,2) represents a number with three places to the left of the decimal and two to the right.
4. **CHAR (n).** Character string n characters long.
5. **DATE.** Dates in the form DD-MON-YY or MM/DD/YYYY. For example, May 12, 1995 could be stored as 12-MAY-95 or as 5/12/1995.

There is another related command that you will need if you happen to enter your CREATE TABLE command incorrectly: DROP TABLE. The command is simply DROP TABLE followed by the name of the table. Thus, to delete the *COMPUTER* table, the command would be:

```
DROP TABLE COMPUTER
```

Suppose, for example, you inadvertently typed *EMPNAME* instead of *MFGNAME* or CHAR(5) instead of CHAR(25) in your CREATE TABLE command and didn't discover it until the command had been executed. Simply delete the table using the DROP TABLE command and then enter the correct CREATE TABLE command. Later on in the text, we will see how to change a variety of aspects concerning a table's structure without having to delete the whole table. For now, however, simply follow the procedure of deleting and then re-creating a table to correct a mistake.

Be aware that this will also delete any data that you have entered into the table. Thus, it's a good idea to check your CREATE TABLE commands carefully and correct any problems before you get to the point of adding data.

NULLS

What Are   Occasionally, when a new row is entered into a database or an existing row is
Nulls?   modified, the values for one or more columns are unknown. They may be merely unavailable for the moment; for example, a PC may not yet have been assigned to an employee. In other cases, these values may never be known; perhaps there is a PC that is never assigned to an employee. SQL handles this problem by allowing us to use a special value to represent the situation where an actual value

is unknown or nonapplicable. This special value is called a **null data value** or simply a **null**. Recall the use of the "-" in the Movies database. For a director who is living, for example, "-" will be in the column for year of death. This is really a null value.

In any system that supports null values, you must choose whether or not to allow them for each column.

Question: Should a user be allowed to enter null values for the primary key?

Answer: It doesn't make sense to allow a user to enter null values for the primary key. For example, the wisdom of storing an employee whose employee number is unknown is questionable at best. Further, if we have stored two such employees, we have no way to distinguish them.

Imple-mentation of Nulls

To support nulls, there must be a mechanism to indicate which columns can contain null values and which cannot. This is accomplished through the clause NOT NULL. Those columns whose description includes NOT NULL are not allowed to accept null values. Other columns may accept such values.

For example, suppose that the employee number and name cannot accept null values but all other columns in the *COMPUTER* table can. The corresponding CREATE TABLE command would be:

```
CREATE TABLE COMPUTER
     (COMPID        DECIMAL(2)  NOT NULL,
      MFGNAME       CHAR(15)    NOT NULL,
      MFGMODEL      CHAR(25),
      PROCTYPE      DECIMAL(7,2))
```

Any attempt to store a null value in either the COMPID or MFGNAME columns will be rejected by the system. An attempt to store a null value in the processor type column, however, will not cause any difficulty.

LOADING A DATABASE

The Basic INSERT Command

Once the tables have been created, we are ready to load the database. To load a database, we add the necessary rows to each table. To add rows, use the INSERT command as shown in the following examples. The only special thing you need to know is that values for character columns must be enclosed in single quote marks (for example, 'Alvarez, Ramon').

Example 2: Add the employee (124, 'Alvarez, Ramon', 1212) to the database.

Note that the character string ('Alvarez, Ramon') is enclosed in single quote marks since it is a value for a character column.

The INSERT command has the form INSERT INTO followed by the name of the table to which we are adding data. Next is the word VALUES followed by the specific values that are to be inserted. In this example, the command would be:

```
INSERT INTO EMPLOYEE
      VALUES
      (124,'Alvarez, Ramon',1212)
```

At this point, the Employee table would contain the data shown in Figure 2.2.

Figure 2.2

EMPLOYEE table with one record inserted

EMPLOYEE

EMPNUM	EMPNAME	EMPPHONE
124	Alvarez, Ramon	1212

Example 3: Add the second and third employees (567, 'Feinstein, Betty', 8716) and (611, 'Dinh, Melissa', 2963) to the database.

We use two INSERT commands to add these sales reps, as follows:

```
INSERT INTO EMPLOYEE
      VALUES
      (567,'Feinstein, Betty',8716)
INSERT INTO EMPLOYEE
      VALUES
      (611,'Dinh, Melissa',2963)
```

Once we have finished, the Employee table contains the data shown in Figure 2.3. Since this is all the data we needed to enter, the table is now loaded.

Figure 2.3

EMPLOYEE table with three records inserted

EMPLOYEE

EMPNUM	EMPNAME	EMPPHONE
124	Alvarez, Ramon	1212
567	Feinstein, Betty	8716
611	Dinh, Melissa	2963

The INSERT Command with Nulls

To enter a null value into a table, we use a special form of the INSERT command. In this form, we identify the names of the columns into which non-null values are being entered. Then we list only these non-null values after the word VALUES, as shown in Example 4.

Example 4: Suppose that when adding data for sales rep 611, Melissa Dinh, as Example 3 shows, we didn't know her phone number. The number should therefore be set to null.

```
INSERT INTO EMPLOYEE (EMPNUM, EMPNAME)
     VALUES
     (611,'Dinh, Melissa')
```

In this command, we are indicating that we are only entering *EMPNUM* and *EMPNAME*. We are *not* entering a value for *EMPPHONE*. Note that no value for *EMPPHONE* is included within the parentheses.

SUMMARY

Following is a summary of the material covered in Chapter 2:

1. To describe a table, use the CREATE TABLE command.
2. The possible data types are INTEGER, SMALLINT, DECIMAL, CHAR, and DATE.
3. A null data value (or simply null) is a special value used when the actual value is unknown.
4. To load data into a database, use the INSERT command.

EXERCISES (CHAZY ASSOCIATES)

1. Use CREATE TABLE commands to describe all the tables in the Chazy Associates database to SQL. The information you will need is shown in Figure 2.4. This information is rather generic (for example, the use of ''Numeric'' for numbers rather than something specific such as DECIMAL, INTEGER, or SMALLINT). Feel free to use any type provided by your implementation of SQL that will allow implementing numbers with the indicated sizes.
2. Add all the employees shown in Figure 1.2 to the *COMPUTER* table using the INSERT command.
3. Add the remaining data shown in Figure 1.2 to the other tables in the Chazy Associates database. You can use the INSERT command for this. If your system has a simpler way to add data, however, feel free to use it.

Data Definition

Figure 2.4

Table layouts for
Chazy Associates
database

COMPUTER

Column	Type	Length	Dec. Places	Nulls Allowed?	Description
COMPID	Char	4			Computer ID (key)
MFGNAME	Char	6			Manufacturer name
MFGMODEL	Char	3			Manufacturer model
PROCTYPE	Char	6			Processor type

EMPLOYEE

Column	Type	Length	Dec. Places	Nulls Allowed?	Description
EMPNUM	Numeric	3	0		Employee number (key)
EMPNAME	Char	10			Employee name
EMPPHONE	Numeric	4		Yes	Employee phone number

PC

Column	Type	Length	Dec. Places	Nulls Allowed?	Description
TAGNUM	Char	5			Tag number (key)
COMPID	Char	4			Computer ID (matches COMPID in COMPUTER table)
EMPNUM	Numeric	3	0		Employee number (matches EMPNUM in EMPLOYEE table)
LOCATION	Char	12		Yes	Location of PC

PACKAGE

Column	Type	Length	Dec. Places	Nulls Allowed?	Description
PACKID	Char	4			Package ID (key)
PACKNAME	Char	20			Package name
PACKVER	Numeric	4	2		Package version
PACKTYPE	Char	15			Package type
PACKCOST	Numeric	6	2		Package cost

SOFTWARE

Column	Type	Length	Dec. Places	Nulls Allowed?	Description
PACKID	Char	4			Package ID (portion of key) (matches PACKID in PACKAGE table)
TAGNUM	Char	5			Tag number (remainder of key) (matches TABNUM in PC table)
INSTDATE	Date				Installation date
SOFTCOST	Numeric	6	2		Software cost (may be different from PACKCOST)

EXERCISES (MOVIES)

1. Use CREATE TABLE commands to describe all the tables in the Movies database to SQL. The information you will need is shown in Figure 2.5. This information is rather generic (for example, the use of "Numeric" for numbers rather than something specific such as DECIMAL, INTEGER, or SMALLINT). Feel free to use any type provided by your implementation of SQL that will allow implementing numbers with the indicated sizes.

Figure 2.5

Table layouts for Movies database

DIRECTOR

Column	Type	Length	Dec. Places	Nulls Allowed?	Description
DIRNUMB	Numeric	3	0		Director number
DIRNAME	Char	18			Director name
DIRBORN	Numeric	4	0		Year of birth
DIRDIED	Numeric	4	0	Yes	Year of death (null if still living)

STAR

Column	Type	Length	Dec. Places	Nulls Allowed?	Description
STARNUMB	Numeric	4	0		Star number
STARNAME	Char	18			Star name
BRTHPLCE	Char	25		Yes	Birthplace
STARBORN	Numeric	4	0		Year of birth
STARDIED	Numeric	4	0	Yes	Year of death (null if still living)

MOVIE

Column	Type	Length	Dec. Places	Nulls Allowed?	Description
MVNUMB	Numeric	4	0		Movie number
MVTITLE	Char	30			Movie title
YRMDE	Numeric	4	0		Year made
MVTYPE	Char	6		Yes	Movie type (COMEDY, SCI FI, SUSPEN, HORROR, DRAMA, RELIGI, WESTER)
CRIT	Numeric	1	0	Yes	Critics' rating (number of stars awarded)
MPAA	Char	2		Yes	MPAA rating (G, PG, etc.)
NOMS	Numeric	1	0	Yes	Number of academy award nominations
AWRD	Numeric	1	0	Yes	Number of academy awards won
DIRNUMB	Numeric	3	0	Yes	Director number (must match DIRNUMB of DIRECTOR table)

Figure 2.5

Table layouts for
Movies database
(continued)

MOVSTAR

Column	Type	Length	Dec. Places	Nulls Allowed?	Description
MVNUMB	Numeric	4	0		Movie number (must match MVNUMB of MOVIE table)
STARNUMB	Numeric	4	0		Star number (must match STARNUMB of STAR table)

MEMBER

Column	Type	Length	Dec. Places	Nulls Allowed?	Description
MMBNUMB	Numeric	4	0		Member number
MMBNAME	Char	16			Member name
MMBADDR	Char	12			Member address (street)
MMBCTY	Char	10			Member city
MMBST	Char	2			Member state
NUMRENT	Numeric	3	0		Number of rentals member has had
BONUS	Numeric	2	0		Number of bonus units member has qualified for but not used
JOINDATE	Date				Date member joined the club

TAPE

Column	Type	Length	Dec. Places	Nulls Allowed?	Description
TPNUMB	Numeric	4	0		Tape number
MVNUMB	Numeric	4	0		Movie number (must match MVNUMB of MOVIE table)
PURDATE	Date				Date tape was purchased
TMSRENT	Numeric	3	0		Number of times tape has been rented
MMBNUMB	Numeric	4	0	Yes	Member number (of the member who is currently renting the tape) Null if tape is not currently being rented.

2. Add all the directors shown in Figure 1.5 to the *DIRECTOR* table using the INSERT command. (Watch out for the nulls. Remember that you must use a special form of the INSERT command.)
3. Add the remaining data shown in Figures 1.6 through 1.10 to the other tables in the Movies database. You can use the INSERT command for this. If your system has a simpler way to add data, however, feel free to use it.

Single-Table Queries

OBJECTIVES

When you have completed this chapter, you should understand the following:

1. The basic form of an SQL command to retrieve data from a database.
2. How to use compound conditions.
3. How to use computed columns.
4. How to use the SQL word LIKE.
5. How to use the SQL word IN.
6. How to sort data using ORDER BY.
7. How to sort with multiple keys and how to sort in descending order.
8. How to use the SQL built-in functions.
9. How to use subqueries.
10. How to group using GROUP BY.
11. How to use HAVING to select individual groups.
12. How to test for nulls.

INTRODUCTION

In this chapter we investigate the SQL SELECT statement, the statement used to access data in a database. We examine the manner in which data can be sorted and use the built-in functions of SQL to count rows and calculate totals. We also discuss ways of using a special feature of SQL that allows SELECT statements to be nested (one SELECT placed inside another). Finally, we see how to group rows that have matching values in some column.

SIMPLE RETRIEVAL

The basic form of an SQL expression is simple: SELECT-FROM-WHERE. After the SELECT, we list those columns that we wish to display. After the FROM, we list the table or tables that are involved in the query. Finally, after the WHERE, we list any conditions that apply to the data we want to retrieve.

There are no special format rules in SQL. In this text, we place the word FROM on a new line indented five spaces and then place the word WHERE (when it is used) on the next line indented five spaces. This makes the commands more readable.

Retrieve Certain Columns and All Rows

Example 5: List the ID, name, and cost of all software packages in the database.

Since we want all packages listed, there is no need for the WHERE clause (we have no restrictions). The query is thus:

```
SELECT PACKID, PACKNAME, PACKCOST
    FROM PACKAGE
```

The computer responds with:

```
PACKID PACKNAME            PACKCOST
AC01   Boise Accounting      725.83
DB32   Manta                 380.00
DB33   Manta                 430.18
SS11   Limitless View        217.95
WP08   Words & More          185.00
WP09   Freeware Processing    30.00
```

Retrieve All Columns and All Rows

Example 6: List the complete PC table.

We could certainly use the same approach as in Example 2. However, there is a shortcut. Instead of listing all the column names after SELECT, we can use the "*" symbol (usually pronounced "star"). This indicates that we want all columns listed (in the order in which we described them to the system during data definition). If we want all the columns, but in a different order, we would have to type the names of the columns in the order in which we want them to appear. In this case, assuming the normal order is appropriate, the query would be:

```
SELECT *
    FROM PC

TAGNUM COMPID EMPNUM LOCATION
32808  M759      611 Accounting
37691  B121      124 Sales
57772  C007      567 Info Systems
59836  B221      124 Home
77740  M759      567 Home
```

Use of the WHERE Clause — Simple Conditions

Example 7: What is the name of employee 124?

We use the WHERE clause to restrict the output of the query to employee 124 as follows:

```
SELECT EMPNAME
    FROM EMPLOYEE
    WHERE EMPNUM = 124


EMPNAME
Alvarez, Ramon
```

The condition in the preceding WHERE clause is called a simple condition. A **simple condition** has the form: column name, comparison operator, then either another column name or a value. The possible comparison operators are shown in Figure 3.1. Note that there are two different versions for "not equal to" (<> and !=). You must use the one that is right for your particular implementation of SQL. (If you use the wrong one, your system will instantly let you know. Then simply switch to the other.)

Figure 3.1

Comparison operators

Comparison Operator	Meaning
=	Equal to
<	Less than
>	Greater than
<=	Less than or equal to
>=	Greater than or equal to
<>	Not equal to (used by most implementations of SQL
!=	Not equal to (used by some implementations of SQL

In Example 7, the WHERE clause compared a numeric column, *EMPNUM*, to a number, 124. In that command, we simply used the number 124. No special action had to be taken. When the query involves a character column, such as *EMPNAME*, the value to which the column is being compared must be surrounded by single quote marks, as Example 8 illustrates.

Example 8: Find the package ID and name for any package whose type is Database.

Since the *PACKTYPE* column is a character column, we need to enclose the word Database in single quote marks. The query is thus:

```
SELECT PACKID, PACKNAME
    FROM PACKAGE
    WHERE PACKTYPE = 'Database'
```

```
PACKID  PACKNAME
DB32    Manta
DB33    Manta
```

Compound Conditions

The conditions we have seen up to this point are called simple conditions. The next examples require compound conditions. **Compound conditions** are formed by connecting two or more simple conditions using AND, OR, and NOT. When simple conditions are connected by the word AND, all the simple conditions must be true in order for the compound condition to be true. When simple conditions are connected by the word OR, the compound condition will be true whenever any of the simple conditions are true. Preceding a condition by the word NOT reverses the truth or falsity of the original condition. That is, if the original condition is true, the new condition will be false; if the original condition was false, the new one will be true.

Example 9: List the IDs and names of all packages whose type is Database and whose cost is over $400.

In this example, we want those packages for which *both* the package type is equal to Database *and* the cost is greater than $400. Thus, we form a compound condition using the word AND as follows:

```
SELECT PACKID, PACKNAME
    FROM PACKAGE
    WHERE PACKTYPE = 'Database'
    AND PACKCOST > 400
```

```
PACKID      PACKNAME
DB33        Manta
```

For readability, we placed each of the simple conditions on a separate line. Some people prefer to put the conditions on the same line with parentheses around each simple condition, as in the following:

```
SELECT PACKNAME
    FROM PACKAGE
    WHERE (PACKTYPE = 'Database') AND (PACKCOST > 400)
```

```
PACKID      PACKNAME
DB33        Manta
```

It is acceptable to use parentheses even when the conditions are on separate lines, as in:

```
SELECT PACKNAME
    FROM PACKAGE
    WHERE (PACKTYPE = 'Database')
    AND (PACKCOST > 400)
```

```
PACKID        PACKNAME
DB33          Manta
```

In what follows, we will place simple conditions on separate lines but will not use parentheses.

Example 10: List the names of all packages whose type is Database or whose cost is over $400.

In this example, we want those packages for which the package type is equal to Database *or* the cost is greater than $400. Thus, we form a compound condition using the word OR as follows:

```
SELECT PACKNAME
    FROM PACKAGE
    WHERE PACKTYPE = 'Database'
    OR PACKCOST > 400

PACKID        PACKNAME
AC01          Boise Accounting
DB32          Manta
DB33          Manta
```

Example 11: List the names of all packages that are not of type Database.

For this example, we could use a simple condition with the condition operator "not equal to." Alternatively, we could use EQUALS in the condition but precede the whole condition with the word NOT, as follows:

```
SELECT PACKNAME
    FROM PACKAGE
    WHERE NOT (PACKTYPE = 'Database')

PACKNAME
Boise Accounting
Limitless View
Words & More
Freeware Processing
```

The condition *PACKTYPE = 'Database'* does not need to be enclosed in parentheses, but doing so makes the command more readable. Note that by phrasing the condition in this form, we have avoided the problem of whether our implementation uses <> or != for not equal to.

Use of BETWEEN

In Example 12, we want to list the ID, name, and cost of all packages whose cost is between $200 and $400. We could certainly do this using a compound condition, as Example 12 illustrates.

Example 12: List the ID, name, and cost of all packages whose cost is between $200 and $400.

Question: How would you do this with a compound condition?

Answer:

```
SELECT PACKID, PACKNAME, PACKCOST
    FROM EMPLOYEE
    WHERE PACKCOST > 200
    AND PACKCOST < 400

PACKID  PACKNAME      PACKCOST
DB32    Manta           380.00
SS11    Limitless View  217.95
```

An alternative to this approach uses the special word BETWEEN as follows:

```
SELECT PACKID, PACKNAME, PACKCOST
    FROM EMPLOYEE
    WHERE PACKCOST BETWEEN 200 AND 400

PACKID  PACKNAME      PACKCOST
DB32    Manta           380.00
SS11    Limitless View  217.95
```

While BETWEEN is not an essential feature of SQL (we have just seen that we can accomplish the same thing without it), it does simplify certain SELECT statements.

Use of Computed Columns

It is possible to use computed columns in SQL queries. By a **computed column**, we mean one that does not exist in the database but that can be computed from columns that do. Such computations can involve any of the arithmetic operators shown in Figure 3.2. The query in Example 13, for example, uses multiplication.

Example 13: Suppose the packages in the database are all to be discounted 10%. List the ID, name, and discounted cost for all packages.

Figure 3.2

Arithmetic operators

Arithmetic Operator	Meaning
=	Addition
-	Subtraction
*	Multiplication
/	Division

There is no column for discounted cost in our database. It is, however, computable from the *PACKCOST* column, since the discounted cost is 90% (.90) multiplied by the package cost. In this case, we would have:

```
SELECT PACKID, PACKNAME, (.90 * PACKCOST)
     FROM PACKAGE


PACKID PACKNAME                    EXP1
AC01   Boise Accounting          653.25
DB32   Manta                     342.00
DB33   Manta                     387.16
SS11   Limitless View            196.16
WP08   Words & More              166.50
WP09   Freeware Processing        27.00
```

The parentheses around the calculation (*.90 * PACKCOST*) are not essential but improve readability.

Note: The heading for the third column in the result is EXP1. This will vary from one implementation of SQL to another. Some will use the expression as the column heading. Still others will simply use the number 3, to indicate it is the third column.

You can use computed fields in comparisons, as Example 14 illustrates.

Example 14: Suppose the packages in the database are all to be discounted 10%. List the ID, name, and discounted cost for all packages whose discounted price is at most $200.

```
SELECT PACKID, PACKNAME, (.90 * PACKCOST)
     FROM PACKAGE
     WHERE (.90 * PACKCOST) <= 200


PACKID PACKNAME                    EXP1
SS11   Limitless View            196.16
WP08   Words & More              166.50
WP09   Freeware Processing        27.00
```

Again, the parentheses around the calculation (*.90 * PACKCOST*) are used to improve readability.

Use of LIKE   **Example 15:** List the ID and name of all packages whose name contains an ampersand (&).

In this case, all we know is that the names of the packages that we want contain a certain character (an ampersand) somewhere within them, but we don't know where. Fortunately, SQL has a facility that we can use in this situation, as the following illustrates:

```
SELECT PACKID, PACKNAME
    FROM PACKAGE
    WHERE PACKNAME LIKE '%&%'

PACKID          PACKNAME
WP08            Words & More
```

The symbol "%" is used as a "wild card." Thus, we are asking for all packages whose name is LIKE some collection of characters, first followed by an ampersand and then by some other characters.

Use of IN   The word IN furnishes a concise way of phrasing certain conditions, as example 16 illustrates. We will see another use for the word IN in more complex examples later in the text.

Example 16: List the ID, name, and type of all packages whose type is Database, Spreadsheet, or Word Processing.

In this query, we will use a new approach to the problem of determining whether a package type is Database, Spreadsheet, or Word Processing using the SQL word IN. We could have obtained the same answer by saying *PACK-TYPE* = 'Database' OR *PACKTYPE* = 'Spreadsheet' OR *PACKTYPE* = 'Word Processing'. This new approach is a little simpler.

```
SELECT PACKID, PACKNAME, PACKTYPE
    FROM PACKAGE
    WHERE PACKTYPE IN ('Database', 'Spreadsheet',
    'Word Processing')

PACKID    PACKNAME              PACKTYPE
DB32      Manta                 Database
DB33      Manta                 Database
SS11      Limitless View        Spreadsheet
WP08      Words & More          Word Processing
WP09      Freeware Processing   Word Processing
```

Here the word IN is followed by a collection of values, in this case, the values 'Database', 'Spreadsheet', and 'Word Processing'. The condition is true for those rows in which the value of *PACKTYPE* is in this collection.

SORTING

Recall that the order of rows in a table is considered to be immaterial. From a practical standpoint, this means that in querying a relational database, there are no guarantees concerning the order in which the results will be displayed. It may be in the order in which the data was originally entered, but even this is not certain. Thus, if the order in which the data is displayed is important, we should *specifically* request that the results be displayed in the desired order. In SQL, this is done with the ORDER BY clause, as Example 17 shows.

Use of ORDER BY

Example 17: List the number, name, and phone of all employees. Order the output by name.

The column on which data is to be sorted is called a **sort key**, or simply a **key**. In this case, since the output is to be ordered (sorted) by name, the key is *EMPNAME*. To sort the output, we include the words ORDER BY, followed by the sort key. Thus, the appropriate query is:

```
SELECT EMPNUM, EMPNAME, EMPPHONE
    FROM EMPLOYEE
    ORDER BY EMPNAME

EMPNUM EMPNAME                EMPPHONE
   124 Alvarez, Ramon            1212
   611 Dinh, Melissa             2963
   567 Feinstein, Betty          8716
```

Sorting with Multiple Keys, Descending Order

Example 18: List the package ID, name, type, and cost. The output should be sorted by package type. (Within a group of packages of the same type, the output is to be sorted by decreasing cost.)

This example involves two new ideas: sorting on multiple keys (package type and cost) and using descending order for one of the keys. To sort on multiple keys, we simply list the keys in order of importance after the words ORDER BY. To sort in descending order, we follow the name of the sort key with DESC. The query is thus:

```
SELECT PACKID, PACKNAME, PACKTYPE, PACKCOST
    FROM PACKAGE
    ORDER BY PACKTYPE, PACKCOST DESC

PACKID  PACKNAME            PACKTYPE          PACKCOST
AC01    Boise               Accounting          725.83
DB33    Manta               Database            430.18
DB32    Manta               Database            380.00
SS11    Limitless View      Spreadsheet         217.95
WP08    Words & More        Word Processing     185.00
WP09    Freeware Processing Word Processing      30.00
```

BUILT-IN FUNCTIONS

SQL has built-in functions to calculate such things as sums, averages, and so on. The list of built-in functions is shown in Figure 3.3.

Figure 3.3

Built-in functions

Built-in Function	Meaning
COUNT	Count of the number of rows satisfying the WHERE clause.
SUM	Sum of the values in a column for all rows satisfying the WHERE clause (column must be numeric).
AVG	Average of the values in a column for all rows satisfying the WHERE clause (column must be numeric).
MAX	Largest value in a column for all rows satisfying the WHERE clause. (If column is numeric, will be largest number. If not, will be highest entry based on collating sequence. If column contains names, for example, will be last name alphabetically.)
MIN	Smallest value in a column for all rows satisfying WHERE clause. (If column is numeric, will be smallest number. If not, will be lowest entry based on collating sequence. If column contains names, for example, will be first name alphabetically.)

Use of the Built-in Function COUNT

Example 19: How many packages are of type Database?

In this query, we're interested in the number of rows in the table produced by selecting only those packages whose type is Database. We could count the number of package IDs in this table, the number of package names, or the number of entries in any other column. It doesn't matter. Rather than requiring us to pick one of these arbitrarily, some versions of SQL allow us to use the "*" symbol. In such a version, we could formulate the query as:

```
SELECT COUNT(*)
    FROM PACKAGE
    WHERE PACKTYPE = 'Database'

    COUNT1
      2
```

If this is not allowed, we would formulate it as:

```
SELECT COUNT(PACKID)
    FROM PACKAGE
    WHERE PACKTYPE = 'Database'

    COUNT1
      2
```

Use of SUM   **Example 20:** Find the number of packages and the total of their costs.

There are two differences between COUNT and SUM, other than the obvious fact that they are computing different statistics.

1. With SUM, we *must* specify the column for which we want the sum calculated.
2. The column must be numeric. (How could you calculate a sum of names or addresses, for example?)

This query is:

```
SELECT COUNT(PACKID), SUM(PACKCOST)
    FROM PACKAGE

    COUNT1          SUM2
        6        1968.96
```

The use of AVG, MAX, and MIN is similar to SUM. The only difference is that a different statistic is calculated. The following illustrates the use of these three functions:

```
SELECT COUNT(PACKID), AVG(PACKCOST)
    FROM PACKAGE

    COUNT1          AVG2
        6         356.32

SELECT COUNT(PACKID), MAX(PACKCOST)
    FROM PACKAGE

    COUNT1          MAX2
        6         725.83

SELECT COUNT(PACKID), MIN(PACKCOST)
    FROM PACKAGE

    COUNT1          MIN2
        6          30.00
```

Note: When you use SUM, AVG, MAX, or MIN, any null values in the column are ignored; that is, they are eliminated from the computation.

Use of   The word DISTINCT is not one of the built-in functions. In some situations,
DISTINCT   however, it can prove useful when used in conjunction with COUNT. Before examining such a situation, we will examine the effect of word DISTINCT. Example 21 illustrates the most common use of DISTINCT.

Example 21: Find the employee numbers of all employees who are currently assigned PCs.

The formulation seems fairly simple. If an employee is currently assigned a PC, there must be at least one row in the *PC* table in which that employee's number appears. Thus, we could say:

```
SELECT EMPNUM
     FROM PC

EMPNUM
   611
   124
   567
   124
   567
```

Note that employees 124 and 567 each appear more than once in the output. The reason for this is that both employees are currently assigned more than one PC and thus their employee numbers appear more than once. Suppose we want to list each such employee only once, as in Example 22.

Example 22: Find the numbers of all employees who are currently assigned PCs. List each employee number exactly once.

This is where the word DISTINCT is used. If we want to ensure uniqueness, we use this word in the following manner:

```
SELECT DISTINCT EMPNUM
     FROM PC

EMPNUM
   124
   567
   611
```

Now let's turn to the relationship between COUNT and DISTINCT.

Example 23: Count the number of employees who are currently assigned PCs.

Question: What's wrong with the following formulation?

```
SELECT COUNT(EMPNUM)
     FROM PC

     COUNT1
       5
```

Answer: The answer (5) is the result of counting the numbers of employees who are assigned PCs once for each PC they are currently assigned.

To overcome this difficulty, we again use the word DISTINCT:

```
SELECT COUNT(DISTINCT EMPNUM)
     FROM PC

     COUNT1
        3
```

NESTING QUERIES

It is possible to place one query inside another. The inner query is called a **subquery** and is executed first. The following example illustrates one of the common uses of subqueries.

Example 24: List the package ID and name for all packages whose cost is greater than the average cost of the database packages.

```
SELECT PACKID, PACKNAME
     FROM PACKAGE
     WHERE PACKCOST >
          (SELECT AVG(PACKCOST)
          FROM PACKAGE
          WHERE PACKTYPE = 'Database')

  PACKID PACKNAME
  AC01   Boise Accounting
  DB33   Manta
```

The portion in parentheses is called a subquery. This subquery is evaluated first, producing a temporary table. In this case, the table has one column called *AVG(PACKCOST)* and a single row containing the number (see Figure 3.4).

The outer query can now be evaluated. We will only obtain the IDs and names of packages whose cost exceeds the result produced by the subquery. Since that table contains only the average package cost for all the packages of type "Database," we will obtain the desired list of packages.

Figure 3.4

Temporary table produced by evaluating subquery

TEMPORARY TABLE

AVG(PACKCOST)
405.09

GROUPING

Example 25: For each PC, list the tag number along with the total value of the software installed on the PC.

Each PC has a particular tag number (*TAGNUM*). To calculate the total value of the software installed on a particular PC, we need to sum the values in the *SOFTCOST* column for all rows in the *SOFTWARE* table containing this tag number for the PC in the *TAGNUM* column.

If we wanted the total for one specific PC—say, the one with tag number 32808—we could use a query such as the following:

```
SELECT SUM(SOFTCOST)
    FROM SOFTWARE
    WHERE TAGNUM = 32808
```

In this example, however, we want to do this for all PCs. The way to do so is to request SQL to *group* the rows in *SOFTWARE* by tag number and then calculate the sum for each group. To do so, we use the GROUP BY clause. In this case, GROUP BY *TAGNUM* will cause the rows for each tag number to be "grouped," that is, all rows with the same tag number will form a group. Any statistics, such as totals, requested in the SELECT clause will be calculated for each of these groups. It is important to note that the GROUP BY clause does not imply that the information will be sorted. To produce the report in a particular order, we need to use the ORDER BY clause. Assuming that the report is to be ordered by tag number, we would have the following formulation:

```
SELECT TAGNUM, SUM(SOFTCOST)
    FROM SOFTWARE
    GROUP BY TAGNUM
    ORDER BY TAGNUM
```

G_TAGNUM	SUM1
32808	1319.95
37691	607.50
57772	583.01
59836	35.00
77740	35.00

When rows are grouped, one line of output is produced for each group. The only things that may be displayed are statistics calculated for the group or columns whose values are the same for all rows in a group.

Q & A

Question: Is it appropriate to display the tag number?

Answer: Yes, since the output is grouped by tag number; thus, the tag number on one row in a group must be the same as the tag number on any other row in the group.

Q & A

Question: Would it be appropriate to display the package ID?

Answer: No, since the package ID will vary from one row in a group to another. (SQL could not determine which part number to display for the group.)

Using HAVING

Example 26: List the tag number and the total value of software for each PC where the value of the software is more than $600.

This example is like the previous one. The only difference is that there is a restriction: namely, we only want to display totals for those PCs with more than $600 worth of software installed on them. This restriction does not apply to individual rows but, rather, to *groups*. Since the WHERE clause applies only to rows, it is not the appropriate clause to accomplish the kind of selection we have here. Fortunately, there is a facility that is to groups what WHERE is to rows. It is the HAVING clause, as shown below:

```
SELECT TAGNUM, SUM(SOFTCOST)
    FROM SOFTWARE
    GROUP BY TAGNUM
    HAVING SUM(SOFTCOST) > 600
    ORDER BY TAGNUM

G_TAGNUM            SUM1
32808            1319.95
37691             607.50
```

In this case, the row created for a group will be displayed only if the sum calculated for the group is larger than $600.

HAVING vs. WHERE

Just as the WHERE clause can be used to limit the *rows* that are included in the result of an SQL command, the HAVING clause can limit the *groups* that are included. The following examples illustrate the differences in these two clauses.

Example 27: List each package type together with the number of packages of that type.

In order to count the number of packages of a given type, the data must by GROUPed BY type. Thus the formulation would be:

```
SELECT PACKTYPE, COUNT(PACKID)
    FROM PACKAGE
    GROUP BY PACKTYPE
```

```
PACKTYPE                COUNT(PACKID)
Accounting                    1
Database                      2
Spreadsheet                   1
Word Processing               2
```

Example 28: Repeat Example 27, but only list those types for which there are more than one package.

Since this condition involves a group total, a HAVING clause is used. The formulation would be:

```
SELECT PACKTYPE, COUNT(PACKID)
    FROM PACKAGE
    GROUP BY PACKTYPE
    HAVING COUNT(PACKID) > 1
```

```
PACKTYPE                COUNT(PACKID)
Database                      2
Word Processing               2
```

Example 29: List each package type together with the number of packages of that type that cost more than $150.

The condition only involves rows, so the WHERE clause is appropriate and the formulation would be:

```
SELECT PACKTYPE, COUNT(PACKID)
    FROM PACKAGE
    WHERE PACKCOST > 150
    GROUP BY PACKTYPE
```

```
PACKTYPE            COUNT(PACKID)
Accounting                      1
Database                        2
Spreadsheet                     1
Word Processing                 1
```

Example 30: Repeat Example 29, but only list those types for which there are more than one package.

Since the conditions involve both rows and groups, both a WHERE clause and a HAVING clause are required and the formulation is:

```
SELECT PACKTYPE, COUNT(PACKID)
    FROM PACKAGE
    WHERE PACKCOST > 150
    GROUP BY PACKTYPE
    HAVING COUNT(PACKID) > 1

PACKTYPE            COUNT(PACKID)
Database                        2
```

In Example 30, rows from the original table will be considered only if the package cost is more than $150. These rows are then grouped by package type and the count is calculated. Only groups for which the calculated count is greater than 1 will be displayed.

NULLS

Sometimes a condition involves a column that can be null, as illustrated in Example 31.

Example 31: List the number and name of all employees whose phone number is null (unknown).

You might expect that the condition should be something like *EMPPHONE = NULL*, but it's actually *EMPPHONE IS NULL*. (To select employees whose phone numbers are not null, we would use the condition *EMPPHONE IS NOT NULL*.) The formulation is:

```
SELECT EMPNUM, EMPNAME
    FROM EMPLOYEE
    WHERE EMPPHONE IS NULL
```

In the current database, no employees have a null phone number and thus none would be retrieved as a result of this query. You will get a chance to work with nulls in a way that does retrieve data in the exercises for the Movies database.

SUMMARY

Following is a summary of the material covered in Chapter 3:

1. The basic form of an SQL command is SELECT-FROM-WHERE. Specify the columns to be listed after the word SELECT (or * for all columns), the list of tables that contain these columns after the word FROM and any conditions after the word WHERE.
2. Simple conditions can involve any of the normal comparison operators $=$, $>$, $>=$, $<$, $<=$, or $<>$ (not equal).
3. Compound conditions are formed by combining simple conditions using the words AND, OR, or NOT.
4. Computed fields can be used in SQL commands by giving the computation in place of a column name.
5. To check for a value in a character column that is similar to a particular string of characters, use the LIKE clause.
6. To check whether a column contains one of a particular set of values, use the IN clause.
7. To sort data, use the ORDER BY clause. Multiple sort keys are listed in order of importance. To sort in descending order, follow the sort key by DESC.
8. SQL contains the built-in functions COUNT, SUM, AVG, MAX, and MIN.
9. To avoid duplicates, either when listing or counting values, precede the column name with the word DISTINCT.
10. One SQL query can be placed inside another. This is called nesting queries. The inner query, called a subquery, is evaluated first.
11. To group data, use the GROUP BY clause.
12. To restrict the output to certain groups, use the HAVING clause.
13. To find rows containing a null value in some column, use the phrase IS NULL in the WHERE clause.

EXERCISES (CHAZY ASSOCIATES)

Use SQL to do the following:

1. Find the employee number and name of all employees.
2. List the complete *COMPUTER* table.
3. Find the model names of all computers with a 486DX processor.
4. Give the tag numbers of those PCs assigned to employee 124 and whose location is "Home."
5. List the computer ID and model name for those computers with a 486DX or a 486DX2 processor.
6. List the tag numbers and computer IDs for those PCs whose location is not "Home."

7. List the tag numbers and package IDs of all software records on which the cost is between $200 and $500 (not including $200 or $500). (Do this two ways.)
8. Give the tag number, package ID, and discounted software cost (software cost times .95) for each software record.
9. Give the tag number, package ID, and discounted software cost for each software record on which the discounted cost is at least $400.
10. List the package IDs and names of all parts whose type is Database or Spreadsheet. Use the word IN in your formulation.
11. Find the numbers and names of any employee whose last name is Feinstein.
12. List all details about packages. Sort the output by package name.
13. List all details about packages. Sort the output by descending package cost within package type.
14. Find out how many packages cost more than $400.
15. Find the average package cost for packages whose type is Word Processing.
16. List the package ID and name for all packages whose cost is more than average.
17. List the average package cost for packages of each type. Then list only the averages for types containing more than one package.

EXERCISES (MOVIES)

Use SQL to do the following:

1. List the numbers, names, and addresses of all members.
2. List the numbers and titles of all movies.
3. List the complete *DIRECTOR* table.
4. List the names of all directors born during or after 1920.
5. List the tape numbers of all tapes that have been rented at least 10 times.
6. List the numbers and titles of all movies that have won at least one Academy Award.
7. List the numbers and titles of all movies whose MPAA rating is PG.
8. List the numbers and titles of all movies whose MPAA rating is PG and that were nominated for at least one Academy Award.
9. List the numbers and titles of all movies that were rated PG or that won at least one Academy Award.
10. List the numbers and titles of all movies that have an MPAA rating. (If a movie does not have a rating, its rating is listed as NR, which stands for not rated.)
11. List the member numbers and names of all members who have rented between 10 and 20 tapes. (Do this two ways.)
12. List the numbers and names of all directors who are still living.
13. List the numbers, names, and ages (year died − year of birth) of all movie stars who are deceased.

14. Find the numbers and names of all directors whose first name is Stanley.
15. List the numbers and titles of all movies whose type is COMEDY, RELIGI, or SUSPEN. Use the word IN in your formulation.
16. List the numbers, names, addresses, and join dates of all members. Sort the output by name.
17. List the numbers, names, addresses, and join dates of all members. Sort the output by city within state.
18. List the numbers, names, addresses, and join dates of all members. Sort the output by join date. List the member who joined most recently first.
19. Find out how many movies are of type SUSPEN.
20. Find out how many movies are of type SUSPEN, the total number of awards for which these movies were nominated, and the total number of awards they won.
21. Count the number of members who are currently renting tapes.
22. Find the maximum number of awards that any movie directed by director 5 was nominated for. Find *all* movies (any director) that won at least as many awards as this maximum. (Do this with two separate queries. Do it with a single query that utilizes a subquery.)
23. List the numbers and names of all members who have rented more tapes than average.
24. For each director, list the director's number and the total number of awards won by movies he or she has directed.
25. Repeat Exercise 24, but only list the directors for whom the total number of awards is at least 4.
26. For each director, list the director's number and the total number of awards won by comedies (movies whose type is COMEDY) he or she has directed.
27. Repeat Exercise 26, but only list the directors for whom the total number of awards is at least 1.

CHAPTER

4

Multiple-Table Queries

OBJECTIVES

When you have completed this chapter, you should understand the following:

1. How to join tables.
2. How to use IN.
3. How to use EXISTS.
4. How to use a subquery within a subquery.

5. How to use an alias.
6. How to join a table to itself.
7. How to perform set operations (union, intersection, and difference).
8. How to use ALL and ANY.

INTRODUCTION

This chapter investigates how to access two or more tables in one SQL statement. We will see how tables can be joined together and how similar results can be obtained using the word IN or the word EXISTS. We will discuss the use of aliases to simplify queries and to join a table to itself. We will also see how the set operations of union, intersection, and difference can be implemented using SQL commands. Finally, we will examine the use of two other special SQL words: ALL and ANY.

QUERYING MULTIPLE TABLES

Joining Two Tables Together

One common way to access data from more than one table is to **join** the tables together; that is, to find rows in the two tables that have identical values in matching columns. This is accomplished through appropriate conditions in the WHERE clause.

Example 32: For each PC, list the tag number and computer ID together with the number and name of the employee to whom the PC has been assigned.

51

Since the tag numbers and computer IDs are in the *PC* table, while the numbers and names of employees are in the *EMPLOYEE* table, we need to access both tables in our SQL command:

1. In the SELECT clause, we indicate all columns we wish to have displayed.
2. In the FROM clause, we list all tables involved in the query.
3. In the WHERE clause, we give the condition that will restrict the data to be retrieved to only those rows from the two tables that match; that is, to the rows that have common values in matching columns.

We have a problem, however. The matching columns are both called *EMPNUM*: There is a column in *PC* called *EMPNUM*, as well as a column in *EMPLOYEE* called *EMPNUM*. In this case, if we mention *EMPNUM*, it will not be clear which one we mean. Therefore it is necessary to **qualify** *EMPNUM*, that is, to specify the version to which column we are referring. We do this by preceding the name of the column with the name of the table and a period. The *EMPNUM* column in the *EMPLOYEE* table is *EMPLOYEE.EMPNUM*. The *EMPNUM* column in the *PC* table is *PC.EMPNUM*. The query is thus:

```
SELECT TAGNUM, COMPID, EMPLOYEE.EMPNUM, EMPNAME
    FROM PC, EMPLOYEE
    WHERE PC.EMPNUM = EMPLOYEE.EMPNUM

TAGNUM COMPID EMPNUM EMPNAME
32808  M759      611 Dinh, Melissa
37691  B121      124 Alvarez, Ramon
57772  C007      567 Feinstein, Betty
59836  B221      124 Alvarez, Ramon
77740  M759      567 Feinstein, Betty
```

Notice that whenever there is potential ambiguity, we *must* qualify the columns involved. It is permissible to qualify other columns as well, even if there is no confusion. Some people prefer to qualify all columns, which is certainly not a bad approach. In this text, we will only qualify columns when it is necessary to do so.

Example 33: For each PC whose location is "Home," list the tag number and computer ID together with the number and name of the employee to whom the PC has been assigned.

In Example 32, the condition in the WHERE clause served only to relate a PC to an employee. While relating a PC to an employee is essential in this example as well, we also want to restrict the output to only those PCs whose location is "Home." This is accomplished by a compound condition, as follows:

```
SELECT TAGNUM, COMPID, EMPLOYEE.EMPNUM, EMPNAME
    FROM PC, EMPLOYEE
    WHERE PC.EMPNUM = EMPLOYEE.EMPNUM
    AND LOCATION = 'Home'

TAGNUM COMPID EMPNUM EMPNAME
59836  B221      124 Alvarez, Ramon
77740  M759      567 Feinstein, Betty
```

Example 34: For each package that has been installed on a PC, find the tag number of the PC, the package ID, the package name, the installation date, the software cost, and the package cost.

A package is considered to be installed if there is a row in the *SOFTWARE* table in which the package appears. To find the tag number, the installation date, and the software cost, we need only examine the *SOFTWARE* table. To find the package name and the package cost, however, we need to look in the *PACKAGE* table to find rows in the *SOFTWARE* table and rows in the *PACKAGE* table that match, that is, rows on which there is the same package ID. This is accomplished as follows:

```
SELECT TAGNUM, SOFTWARE.PACKID, PACKNAME, INSTDATE,
       SOFTCOST, PACKCOST
    FROM SOFTWARE, PACKAGE
    WHERE SOFTWARE.PACKID = PACKAGE.PACKID
```

TAGNUM	PACKID	PACKNAME	INSTDATE	SOFTCOST	PACKCOST
32808	AC01	Boise Accounting	09/13/95	754.95	725.83
32808	DB32	Manta	12/03/95	380.00	380.00
37691	DB32	Manta	06/15/95	380.00	380.00
57772	DB33	Manta	05/27/95	412.77	430.18
33808	WP08	Words & More	01/12/96	185.00	185.00
37691	WP08	Words & More	06/15/95	227.50	185.00
57772	WP08	Words & More	05/27/95	170.24	185.00
59836	WP09	Freeware Processing	10/30/95	35.00	30.00
77740	WP09	Freeware Processing	05/27/95	35.00	30.00

Comparison of JOIN, IN, and EXISTS

Tables are typically joined in SQL by including a comparison in the WHERE clause to ensure that matching columns have equal values (for example, *SOFTWARE.PACKID = PACKAGE.PACKID*). Similar results can be obtained using either the word IN (which we have seen before) or the word EXISTS together with a subquery. The choice is largely a matter of personal preference. The following examples illustrate the difference.

Example 35: Find the names of all packages installed on the PC with tag number 32808.

Since this query also involves the SOFTWARE and PACKAGE tables, as did Example 34, we could approach it in a similar fashion. There are two basic differences: this query does not require as many fields, and we are only interested in the PC with the tagnum 32808. The fact that there are fewer columns only means there are going to be fewer attributes listed in the SELECT clause. Restriction of the query to a single order is accomplished by adding the condition *TAGNUM* = 32808 to the WHERE clause. Thus one formulation of this query would be:

```
SELECT PACKNAME
    FROM SOFTWARE, PACKAGE
    WHERE SOFTWARE.PACKID = PACKAGE.PACKID
    AND TAGNUM = '32808'

PACKNAME
Boise Accounting
Manta
```

Notice that *SOFTWARE* was listed in the FROM clause even though no fields from the *SOFTWARE* table were to be displayed. Fields from this table were mentioned in the WHERE clause, however, so it was involved in the query.

Using IN

Another approach uses the word IN and a subquery. We could first use a subquery to find all of the package IDs in the *SOFTWARE* table that appear on any row in which the tag number is 32808. Next we find the names of any packages whose package ID is in this list. The formulation to do this is:

```
SELECT PACKNAME
    FROM PACKAGE
    WHERE PACKID IN
        (SELECT PACKID
            FROM SOFTWARE
            WHERE TAGNUM = '32808')

PACKNAME
Boise Accounting
Manta
```

Here, evaluating the subquery produced the temporary table shown in Figure 4.1. Note that this table consists solely of those package IDs (AC01, DB32, and WP08)

Figure 4.1

Temporary table produced by evaluating subquery

TEMPORARY TABLE

```
PACKID
─────────────
AC01
DB32
WP08
```

that are installed on the PC with tag number 32808. Executing the remaining portion of the query produces names of the appropriate packages.

Using   **Example 36:** Find the tag number and computer ID of all PCs on which package
EXISTS   WP08 has been installed.

The query is similar to that in Example 35 but involves the *PC* table instead of the *PACKAGE* table. It could be handled in either of the ways we just discussed. Using the formulation involving IN would give:

```
SELECT TAGNUM, COMPID
     FROM PC
     WHERE TAGNUM IN
           (SELECT TAGNUM
                 FROM SOFTWARE
                 WHERE PACKID = 'WP08')

 TAGNUM COMPID
 37691  B121
 57772  C007
```

The word EXISTS furnishes another way to approach the problem. Use it as follows:

```
SELECT TAGNUM, COMPID
     FROM PC
     WHERE EXISTS
          (SELECT *
               FROM SOFTWARE
               WHERE PC.TAGNUM = SOFTWARE.TAGNUM
               AND PACKID = 'WP08')

 TAGNUM COMPID
 37691  B121
 57772  C007
```

This is the first subquery we have seen that involves a table mentioned in the outer query. Such a subquery is called a **correlated subquery**. In this case, the *PC* table, which occurs in the FROM clause of the outer query, is used in the subquery (*PC.TAGNUM*). (This is why we need to qualify *TAGNUM* in the subquery. We did not need to do so in the queries involving IN.)

This query works as follows. For each row in the *PACKAGE* table, the subquery will be executed using the value of *PC.TAGNUM* that occurs on that row. The inner query will produce a list of all rows in *SOFTWARE* on which *SOFT-WARE.TAGNUM* matches this value and *PACKID* is equal to WP08. This is the point where the word EXISTS is used. Placing EXISTS in front of a subquery gives a condition that is true if one or more rows are obtained when the subquery is executed and false otherwise.

To illustrate the process, consider two PCs, the ones with tag numbers 32808 and 59836. The PC with tag number 32808 will be included in the result since a row exists in *SOFTWARE* with this tag number and package WP08. This makes the EXISTS condition true. The PC with tag number 59836, however, will not be included since no row exists in *SOFTWARE* with this order number and package WP08. Thus, the EXISTS condition is false.

Question: How would you find the tag number and computer ID of all PCs on which package WP08 has not been installed?

Answer: Do this using either of the following:

```
SELECT TAGNUM, COMPID
     FROM PC
     WHERE TAGNUM NOT IN
         (SELECT TAGNUM
               FROM SOFTWARE
               WHERE PACKID = 'WP08')
```

Here, the subquery is selecting all tag numbers from *SOFTWARE* on which the package ID is WP08, as before. The only difference is that this time we are asking for those rows from the *PC* table for which the tag number is *not* in this collection. We could also use NOT EXISTS:

```
SELECT TAGNUM, COMPID
     FROM PC
     WHERE NOT EXISTS
         (SELECT *
               FROM SOFTWARE
               WHERE PC.TAGNUM = SOFTWARE.TAGNUM
               AND PACKID = 'WP08')
```

Here, for each tag number in the *PC* table, the subquery is selecting those rows of the *SOFTWARE* table on which the tag number matches the tag number from the *PC* table and the package ID is WP08. If the tag number from the *PC* table does not appear on any row in *SOFTWARE* on which the package ID is WP08, the result of the subquery will be an empty table. In this case, the NOT EXISTS condition will be true (no rows exist in the table created by the subquery), and this tag number and corresponding computer ID will be printed. If package WP08 has been installed on the PC, there will be at least one row in the table created by the subquery and the NOT EXISTS condition will be false, so the tag number would not be displayed.

**Subquery
within a
Subquery**

Example 37: Find the tag number and computer ID of all PCs on which a package whose type is Database has been installed.

One way to approach this problem is first to determine the list of package IDs in the *PACKAGE* table for those packages whose type is Database. Once this has been done, we can obtain a list of tag numbers in the *SOFTWARE* table whose corresponding package ID is in our package ID list. Finally, we can retrieve the tag numbers and computer IDs in the *PC* table for which the tag number is in the list of tag numbers obtained during the second step. This approach would be formulated in SQL as follows:

```
SELECT TAGNUM, COMPID
     FROM PC
     WHERE TAGNUM IN
          (SELECT TAGNUM
               FROM SOFTWARE
               WHERE PACKID IN
                    (SELECT PACKID
                          FROM PACKAGE
                          WHERE PACKTYPE = 'Database'))

TAGNUM COMPID
 32808 M759
 37691 B121
 57772 C007
```

As you would expect, the queries are evaluated from the innermost query to the outermost query. Thus, this query is evaluated in three steps:

1. The innermost query is evaluated first, producing the table of package IDs for those packages whose type is Database (see Figure 4.2).

Figure 4.2

Temporary table
produced by
evaluating
innermost
subquery

TEMPORARY TABLE

PACKID
DB32
DB33

2. The next subquery is evaluated, producing a list of tag numbers (see Figure 4.3). Each tag number in this collection has a row in *SOFTWARE* on which the package ID is in the temporary table produced in step 1.
3. Finally, the outermost query is evaluated, producing the desired list of tag numbers and computer IDs. Only those PCs whose tag numbers are in the temporary table produced in step 2 will be included.

Figure 4.3	**TEMPORARY TABLE**

Temporary table
produced by
evaluating next
subquery

TAGNUM
```
32808
37691
57772
```

An alternative formulation involves joining three tables, *PC*, *SOFTWARE*, and *PACKAGE*. This formulation is:

```
SELECT PC.TAGNUM, COMPID
    FROM SOFTWARE, PC, PACKAGE
    WHERE SOFTWARE.TAGNUM = PC.TAGNUM
    AND SOFTWARE.PACKID = PACKAGE.PACKID
    AND PACKTYPE = 'Database'

TAGNUM COMPID
 32808 M759
 37691 B121
 57772 C007
```

In this case, the condition *SOFTWARE.TAGNUM = PC.TAGNUM* and the condition *SOFTWARE.PACKID = PACKAGE.PACKID* accomplish the appropriate joining of the tables. The condition *PACKTYPE* = 'Database' restricts the output to only those packages whose type is Database.

The response produced will be correct, regardless of which formulation is used. Thus, the user can employ whichever approach is more comfortable.

You may wonder whether one approach will be more efficient than the other. Good mainframe computer systems have built-in optimizers that analyze queries to determine the best way to satisfy them. Given that your mainframe has a good optimizer, it should not matter how you formulate the query. If you are using a system without such an optimizer, such as one of the many microcomputer database management systems (DBMSs), the formulation of a query can make a difference. In such a case, if efficiency is a prime concern, you should consult the manual for your DBMS.

A Comprehensive Example

Example 38: List the tag number, the computer ID, the employee number, and the total value of installed software for all PCs on which the total value is over $100. Order the results by tag number.

This query involves several of the features already discussed. The formulation is:

```
SELECT PC.TAGNUM, COMPID, EMPNUM, SUM(SOFTCOST)
    FROM PC, SOFTWARE
    WHERE PC.TAGNUM = SOFTWARE.TAGNUM
```

```
GROUP BY PC.TAGNUM, COMPID, EMPNUM
HAVING SUM(SOFTCOST) > 100
ORDER BY PC.TAGNUM
```

TAGNUM	COMPID	EMPNUM	SUM1
32808	M759	611	1134.95
37691	B121	124	607.50
57772	C007	567	583.01

This example illustrates all the major clauses that can be used in the SELECT command. It also shows the order in which these clauses must appear.

In this example, the *PC* and *SOFTWARE* tables are joined by listing both tables in the FROM clause and relating them in the WHERE clause. Data selected is sorted by *TAGNUM*, using the ORDER BY clause. The GROUP BY clause indicates that the data is to be grouped by tag number, computer ID, and employee number. For each group, SELECT indicates that the tag number, computer ID, employee number, and total software cost (SUM(*SOFTCOST*)) are to be displayed. Not all groups will be displayed, however. The HAVING clause indicates that only groups for which the SUM(*SOFTCOST*) is greater than 100 are to be printed.

Notice that for each row, the tag number, computer ID, and employee number are the same. Thus, it would seem that merely grouping by tag number should be sufficient. Most implementations of SQL, however, still require that both computer ID and employee number and date also be listed in the GROUP BY clause. Recall that SELECT can only include statistics calculated for groups or columns whose values are known to be the same for each row in a group. By stating that the data is to be grouped by tag number, computer ID, and employee number, you tell the system that the values of these columns must be the same for each row in a group. A more sophisticated implementation would realize that, given the structure of this database, grouping by tag number alone is sufficient to ensure the uniqueness of both computer ID and employee number.

USING AN ALIAS

When tables are listed in the FROM clause, it is possible to give each table an **alias**, or alternate name, that can be used throughout the rest of the statement. This is done by immediately following the name of the table with the alias. No commas separate the two because commas would make SQL assume that the alias was, in fact, the name of another table.

There are two basic uses for aliases. One is simplicity. In the following example, we will assign the *PC* table the alias P and the *EMPLOYEE* table the alias E. By doing this, we can type P instead of PC and E instead of EMPLOYEE in the remainder of the query. The query is relatively simple, so you may not see the full benefit of this feature. For a very involved query, however, this feature can ease the process greatly.

Example 39: For each PC, list the tag number and computer ID, together with the number and name of the employee to whom the PC has been assigned.

```
SELECT TAGNUM, COMPID, E.EMPNUM, EMPNAME
    FROM PC P, EMPLOYEE E
    WHERE P.EMPNUM = E.EMPNUM
```

```
TAGNUM COMPID EMPNUM EMPNAME
 32808  M759     611 Dinh, Melissa
 37691  B121     124 Alvarez, Ramon
 57772  C007     567 Feinstein, Betty
 59836  B221     124 Alvarez, Ramon
 77740  M759     567 Feinstein, Betty
```

In addition to their role in simplifying queries, aliases are essential in certain situations. We'll see this in Example 40.

MORE INVOLVED JOINS

Joining a Table to Itself

Example 40: Find any pairs of packages that have the same name.

If we had two different tables of packages and the query asked us to find packages in the first table that have the same name as packages in the second table, this would be a regular join operation. Here, however, there is only one table, *PACKAGE*. We can treat it as two tables in the query by using the alias feature of SQL presented in Example 39.

In the FROM clause, we state:

```
FROM PACKAGE FIRST, PACKAGE SECOND
```

As far as SQL is concerned, we are requesting the querying of two tables, one that has the alias FIRST and another that has the alias SECOND. The fact that both tables are really the single table *PACKAGE* is not a problem. Thus, the query could be formulated:

```
SELECT FIRST.PACKID, FIRST.PACKNAME, SECOND.PACKID,
    SECOND.PACKNAME
    FROM PACKAGE FIRST, PACKAGE SECOND
    WHERE FIRST.PACKNAME = SECOND.PACKNAME
    AND FIRST.PACKID < SECOND.PACKID
```

```
PACKID PACKNAME          PACKID PACKNAME
DB32   Manta             DB33   Manta
```

We are requesting a package ID and name from the *FIRST* table, followed by a package ID and name from the *SECOND* table, subject to two conditions: the names must match, and the package ID from the first table must be less than the package ID from the second table.

Question: Why did we include the condition *FIRST.PACKID < SECOND.PACKID*?

Answer: If we did not include this condition, we would get a result such as the following:

```
SELECT FIRST.PACKID, FIRST.PACKNAME, SECOND.PACKID,
    SECOND.PACKNAME
    FROM PACKAGE FIRST, PACKAGE SECOND
    WHERE FIRST.PACKNAME = SECOND.PACKNAME

PACKID PACKNAME                 PACKID PACKNAME
AC01   Boise Accounting         AC01   Boise Accounting
DB32   Manta                    DB32   Manta
DB32   Manta                    DB33   Manta
DB33   Manta                    DB32   Manta
DB33   Manta                    DB33   Manta
SS11   Limitless View           SS11   Limitless View
WP08   Words & More             WP08   Words & More
WP09   Freeware Processing      WP09   Freeware Processing
```

An Example Involving Joining All Five Tables

Example 41: For each installed package, list the package ID, the package name, the installation date, the tag number of the PC on which it was installed, the computer ID of the PC, the number of the employee to whom the PC is assigned, and the name of the employee.

A package is installed if it occurs on any row in the *SOFTWARE* table. The package ID, install date, and the tag number of the PC are all found within the *SOFTWARE* table. If these were the only things required for the query, we could just enter:

```
SELECT PACKID, INSTDATE, TAGNUM
    FROM SOFTWARE
```

This is not all we need, however. We also must have the package name, which is in the *PACKAGE* table; the computer ID and employee number, which are in the *PC* table; and the employee name, which is in the *EMPLOYEE* table. Thus, we really need to join *four* tables: *SOFTWARE*, *PC*, *EMPLOYEE*, and *COMPUTER*. The mechanism for doing this is essentially the same as the mechanism for joining two tables. The only difference is that the condition in the WHERE clause will be a compound condition. The WHERE clause in this case would be:

```
WHERE PACKAGE.PACKID = SOFTWARE.PACKID
AND    PC.TAGNUM = SOFTWARE.TAGNUM
AND    EMPLOYEE.EMPNUM = PC.EMPNUM
```

The first condition relates a package to a software record with a matching package ID. The second condition relates this software record to the PC with a matching tag number. The final condition matches this PC with an employee by using matching employee numbers.

For the complete query, we list all the desired columns after SELECT, qualifying any that appear in more than one table. After FROM, we list all four tables that are involved in the query. The complete formulation is:

```
SELECT SOFTWARE.PACKID, PACKNAME, INSTDATE, SOFTWARE.TAGNUM,
     COMPUTER.COMPID, PC.EMPNUM, EMPNAME
     FROM SOFTWARE, PACKAGE, PC, EMPLOYEE
     WHERE PACKAGE.PACKID = SOFTWARE.PACKID
     AND    PC.TAGNUM = SOFTWARE.TAGNUM
     AND    EMPLOYEE.EMPNUM = PC.EMPNUM
```

PACKID	PACKNAME	INSTDATE	TAGNUM	COMPID	EMPNUM	EMPNAME
AC01	Boise Accounting	09/13/95	32808	M759	611	Dinh, Melissa
DB32	Manta	12/03/95	32808	M759	611	Dinh, Melissa
DB32	Manta	06/15/95	37691	B121	124	Alvarez, Ramon
WP08	Words & More	06/15/95	37691	B121	124	Alvarez, Ramon
DB33	Manta	05/27/95	57772	C007	567	Feinstein, Betty
WP08	Words & More	05/27/95	57772	C007	567	Feinstein, Betty
WP09	Freeware Processing	10/30/95	59836	B221	124	Alvarez, Ramon
WP09	Freeware Processing	05/27/95	77740	M759	567	Feinstein, Betty

Q & A

Question: Could *EMPLOYEE.EMPNUM* be used in place of *PC.EMPNUM* in the SELECT line of the query?

Answer: Yes, since the values for these two columns must match by virtue of the condition *EMPLOYEE.EMPNUM = PC.EMPNUM*. We could choose either one.

Certainly, this last query is more involved than many of the previous ones. You may be thinking that SQL is not such an easy language to use after all. If you take it one step at a time, however, the query really isn't that difficult. To construct the query in a step-by-step fashion, do the following:

1. List all the columns that you want printed on the report after the word SELECT. If the name of any column appears in more than one table, precede the column name with the table name (that is, qualify it).
2. List all the tables involved in the query after the word FROM. Ths will usually be the tables that contain the columns listed in the SELECT clause. Occasionally, however, there might be a table that does not include any columns used in the SELECT clause but does contain columns used in the WHERE clause. It must also be listed. For example, if there were no need to list a computer ID or location, but we had to list the employee name, no columns from the *PC* table would be used in the SELECT clause. The *PC* table would still be required, however, since columns from it must be used in the WHERE clause.
3. Taking the tables involved one pair at a time, put the condition that relates the tables in the WHERE clause. Join these conditions with AND. If there are any other conditions, include them in the WHERE clause and connect them to the others with the word AND. In this example, if we only wanted to include software whose cost was more than $100, we would add one more condition to the WHERE clause:

```
SELECT SOFTWARE.PACKID, PACKNAME, INSTDATE, SOFTWARE.TAGNUM,
       COMPUTER.COMPID, PC.EMPNUM, EMPNAME
       FROM SOFTWARE, PACKAGE, PC, EMPLOYEE
       WHERE PACKAGE.PACKID = SOFTWARE.PACKID
       AND   PC.TAGNUM = SOFTWARE.TAGNUM
       AND   EMPLOYEE.EMPNUM = PC.EMPNUM
       AND   SOFTCOST > 100
```

SET OPERATIONS

In SQL, we can use the normal set operations: union, intersection, and difference. The **union** of two tables is a table containing all rows that are in either the first table or the second or both. The **intersection** of two tables is a table containing all rows that are in both tables. The **difference** of two tables A and B (referred to as A minus B) is the set of all rows that are in Table A but are not in Table B.

There is an obvious restriction on these operations. It does not make sense, for example, to talk about the union of the *COMPUTER* table and the *PACKAGE* table. What would rows in this union look like? The two tables *must* have the same structure. The formal term is *union-compatible*. Two tables are **union-compatible** if they have the same number of columns and if their corresponding columns have identical data types and lengths.

Notice that the definition does not state that the column headings of the two tables must be identical but, rather, that the columns must be of the same type. Thus, if one is CHAR(20), the other must also be CHAR(20).

Union

Example 42: List the computer ID and manufacturer's name of all computers that either have a 486DX processor or have been assigned for home use, or both.

We can create a table containing the ID and manufacturer's name of all computers with a 486DX processor by selecting them from the *COMPUTER* table. Then we can create another table containing the ID and manufacturer's name of all computers assigned to home use by joining the *COMPUTER* table and the *PC* table. The two tables created by this process have the same structure. They each have two columns, an ID and a manufacturer's name. Since the tables are thus union-compatible, we can take the union of them. This is accomplished in SQL by:

```
SELECT COMPID, MFGNAME
     FROM COMPUTER
     WHERE PROCTYPE = '486DX'
UNION
SELECT COMPUTER.COMPID, MFGNAME
     FROM COMPUTER, PC
     WHERE COMPUTER.COMPID = PC.COMPID
     AND LOCATION = 'Home'

 COMPID MFGNAME
 B121   Bantam
 B221   Bantam
 C007   Cody
 M759   Lemmin
```

If an implementation truly supports the union operation, it will remove any duplicate rows (that is, any computers with a 486DX processor that are also assigned to a home). Some implementations of SQL have a "union" operation but will not remove such duplicates.

Intersection

Example 43: List the computer ID and manufacturer's name of all computers that have a 486DX processor and have been assigned for home use.

Here we want the intersection of the table of computers with a 486DX processor and the table of compuaters that have been assigned for home use. The simplest way to do so is to select the computer ID and manufacturer's name of those computers with a 486DX processor *and* that are also in the set of computers that have been assigned for home use. This can be accomplished with the word IN and a subquery as follows:

```
SELECT COMPID, MFGNAME
     FROM COMPUTER
     WHERE PROCTYPE = '486DX'
     AND COMPID IN
     (SELECT COMPID
          FROM PC
          WHERE LOCATION = 'Home')
```

```
COMPID MFGNAME
B221   Bantam
M759   Lemmin
```

Difference   **Example 44:** List the computer ID and manufacturer's name of all computers that have a 486DX processor but have not been assigned for home use.

This query is similar to the previous one. Here, however, we want a difference rather than an intersection. In this case, we want the difference between the table of computers with a 486DX processor and the table of computers that have been assigned for home use. This can be accomplished by simply preceding the word IN in the previous SQL query with the word NOT, as follows:

```
SELECT COMPID, MFGNAME
    FROM COMPUTER
    WHERE PROCTYPE = '486DX'
    AND COMPID IN
        (SELECT COMPID
            FROM PC
            WHERE LOCATION = 'Home')
```

```
COMPID MFGNAME
B121   Bantam
C007   Cody
```

ALL AND ANY

The words ALL and ANY may be used with subqueries that produce a single column of numbers. If the subquery is preceded by the word ALL, the condition will only be true if it is satisfied by *all* values produced by the subquery. If the subquery is preceded by the word ANY, the condition will be true if it is satisfied by *any* (one or more) values produced by the subquery. The next examples illustrate the use of these words.

Using ALL   **Example 45:** Find the package ID, tag number, installation date, and software cost of those software records on which the cost is larger than the package cost of every package in the *PACKAGE* table.

While this query can be satisfied by finding the maximum cost of all packages in a subquery and then finding all software records on which the cost is greater than this number, there is an alternative. Use the word ALL, as in the following query:

```
SELECT PACKID, TAGNUM, INSTDATE, SOFTCOST
    FROM SOFTWARE
    WHERE SOFTCOST > ALL
        (SELECT PACKCOST
            FROM PACKAGE)
```

```
PACKID TAGNUM INSTDATE SOFTCOST
AC01   32808  09/13/95   754.95
```

To some users, this formulation might seem more natural than finding the maximum balance in the subquery. For other users, the opposite might be true. You can employ whichever approach you find more comfortable.

Using ANY

Example 46: Find the package ID, tag number, installation date, and software cost of those software records on which the cost is larger than the package cost of at least one package in the *PACKAGE* table.

This query can be satisfied by finding the minimum cost of all packages in a subquery and then finding all software records on which the cost is greater than this number. Again, there is an alternative. Use the word ANY, as in the following query:

```
SELECT PACKID, TAGNUM, INSTDATE, SOFTCOST
     FROM SOFTWARE
     WHERE SOFTCOST > ANY
           (SELECT PACKCOST
                 FROM PACKAGE)
```

```
PACKID TAGNUM INSTDATE SOFTCOST
AC01   32808  09/13/95   754.95
DB32   32808  12/03/95   380.00
DB32   37691  06/15/95   380.00
DB33   57772  05/27/95   412.77
WP08   33808  01/12/96   185.00
WP08   37691  06/15/95   227.50
WP08   57772  05/27/95   170.24
WP09   59836  10/30/95    35.00
WP09   77740  05/27/95    35.00
```

SUMMARY

Following is a summary of the material covered in Chapter 4:

1. To join tables together, include all tables to be joined after the word FROM as well as conditions requiring values in matching columns to be equal after the word WHERE.
2. Using the word IN or the word EXISTS with an appropriate subquery is an alternative way of performing a join.
3. A subquery may itself contain a subquery. The innermost subquery is executed first.
4. The name of a table in a FROM clause may be followed by an alias, that is, an alternate name for the table. Throughout the remainder of the SQL command, the alias may be used in place of the table name.

5. By using two different aliases for the same table in a single SQL command, a table may be joined to itself.
6. Two tables are union-compatible if they have the same number of columns and if their corresponding columns have identical data types and lengths.
7. The UNION command creates the union of two tables, that is, the collection of rows that are in either of the tables. The tables must be union-compatible.
8. If a subquery is preceded by the word ALL, the condition will only be true if it is satisfied by *all* values produced by the subquery.
9. If a subquery is preceded by the word ANY, the condition will be true if it is satisfied by *any* (one or more) values produced by the subquery.

EXERCISES (CHAZY ASSOCIATES)

Use SQL to do the following:

1. For each PC, list the tag number and computer ID along with the name of the computer manufacturer.
2. For each PC assigned to employee 124, list the tag number and computer ID along with the name of the computer manufacturer.
3. For each PC, list the tag number and computer ID. In addition, for each software package installed on the PC, list the package ID, the package name, and the date of installation.
4. Find the numbers and names of all employees who are assigned a PC for home use (that is, the location is "Home"). Do this in two ways. First, use the word IN; second, use the word EXISTS.
5. Find the numbers and names of all employees who are not assigned a PC for home use.
6. For each PC, list the tag number and computer ID, as well as the name, version, and type of all packages installed on the PC.
7. Find the manufacturer names and models of all PCs that are assigned to at least one employee who uses the computer at home.
8. Find the tag number and computer IDs for those PCs that have at least one database package installed on it. Do this in two ways. In one solution, use a subquery; in the other, do not.
9. List the package IDs and names of pairs of packages that are of the same type.
10. List the tag numbers and computer IDs of any PCs assigned to Ramon Alvarez (Alvarez, Ramon) that have a database package installed on them.
11. List the tag numbers and computer IDs of any PCs assigned to Ramon Alvarez that do not have a database package installed on them.
12. List the tag numbers and computer IDs of any PCs assigned to Ramon Alvarez or that have a database package installed on them.
13. List the package ID and name for all packages that have a package cost greater than the package cost of any package whose type is Database. Use either the

word ALL or the word ANY in your command. (*Hint:* Be careful about which one you use.)

14. If you used ALL in Exercise 13, change it to ANY. If you used ANY, change it to ALL. Once you have done this, run the new command. What question is this command answering?

EXERCISES (MOVIES)

Use SQL to do the following:

1. For each movie, list the movie number and title along with the number and name of the director of the movie.
2. For each tape, list the tape number and purchase date along with the number and title of the movie on the tape.
3. For each movie of type COMEDY, list the movie number and title along with the number and name of the director of the movie.
4. For each tape that has been rented at least five times, list the tape number and purchase date along with the number and title of the movie on the tape.
5. For each tape that is currently rented, list the tape number and the movie number as well as the number and name of the member who is currently renting the tape.
6. Find the numbers and names of all directors who have directed at least one comedy. Do this in two ways. First, use the word IN; second, use the word EXISTS.
7. Find the numbers and names of all directors who have never directed a comedy (at least, as far as the data in this database indicates).
8. For each movie, list the title of the movie together with the names and birthplaces of all the stars who appeared in the movie.
9. List the numbers and names of all stars in the database who have appeared in at least one comedy. Do this in two ways. In one solution, use a subquery; in the other, do not.
10. List the numbers and names of all stars who have appeared in any movies directed by Alfred Hitchcock. (*Hint:* Remember that director names are stored with the last name first. Thus, you must search for Hitchcock, Alfred, for example.)
11. List the numbers and names of any pairs of movies that are of the same type and have the same director.
12. For each movie, list the title, director's name, and the names of all the stars who appeared in the movie.
13. List the tape number and movie number for all tapes on which the movie is a comedy and that are currently rented by Mark Peterson (Peterson, Mark).
14. List the tape number and movie number for all tapes on which the movie is a comedy or that are rented by Mark Peterson.

15. List the tape number and movie number for all tapes on which the movie is a comedy but are currently rented by someone other than Mark Peterson.

16. List the movie number and title for all movies that were nominated for more Academy Awards than any movies directed by Woody Allen. Use either the word ALL or the word ANY in your command. (*Hint*: Be careful about which one you use.)

17. If you used ALL in Exercise 16, change it to ANY. If you used ANY, change it to ALL. Once you have done this, run the new command. What question is this command answering?

Updates

OBJECTIVES

When you have completed this chapter, you should understand the following:

1. How to change data using UPDATE.
2. How to add new data using INSERT.
3. How to delete data using DELETE.
4. How to create a new table from an existing table.
5. How to use nulls in update commands.
6. How to change the structure of a database.

INTRODUCTION

This chapter examines how to make changes in a database. We will learn how to use the UPDATE command to change data in one or more rows in a table, how to use the INSERT command to add new rows, and how to use the DELETE command to delete rows. We will discuss how to create a new table from an existing table and how to use nulls in update operations. Finally, we will see how to change the structure of a database.

Note: Each of the examples in this chapter will make a change to the Chazy Associates database. You will get a chance to make similar changes in the exercises at the end of the chapter. If, however, you wish to execute the commands in the examples as you follow along through the chapter, you should first make a copy (often called a backup) of the Chazy Associates database. That way, after you have made the changes, you will be able to restore the database to its original state simply by copying this backup over the active version.

71

CHANGING EXISTING DATA

Changing Existing Data in the Database

Example 47: Change the name of package DB33 to 'MANTA II'.

The SQL command to make changes to existing data is the UPDATE command. The formulation is:

```
UPDATE PACKAGE
     SET PACKNAME = 'MANTA II'
     WHERE PACKID = 'DB33'
```

After the word UPDATE, we list the table to be updated. The SET clause indicates the column or columns to be changed as well as the new value. The WHERE clause gives the condition that indicates which row or rows are to be changed. The results of this particular command are shown in Figure 5.1.

Figure 5.1

Name has been changed

Before:

PACKAGE

PACKID	PACKNAME	PACKVER	PACKTYPE	PACKCOST
AC01	Boise Accounting	3.00	Accounting	725.83
DB32	Manta	1.50	Database	380.00
DB33	Manta	2.10	Database	430.18
SS11	Limitless View	5.30	Spreadsheet	217.95
WP08	Words & More	2.00	Word Processing	185.00
WP09	Freeware Processing	4.27	Word Processing	30.00

After:

PACKAGE

PACKID	PACKNAME	PACKVER	PACKTYPE	PACKCOST
AC01	Boise Accounting	3.00	Accounting	725.83
DB32	Manta	1.50	Database	380.00
DB33	Manta II	2.10	Database	430.18
SS11	Limitless View	5.30	Spreadsheet	217.95
WP08	Words & More	2.00	Word Processing	185.00
WP09	Freeware Processing	4.27	Word Processing	30.00

Using a Compound Condition

Example 48: For each package of type Database whose cost is over $400, increase the cost by 2%.

There are two differences between this example and Example 47. First, the SET clause includes a computation that involves the previous value in the field. (The new value of package cost should be the previous value multiplied by

1.02.) The other difference is that the condition is compound. Here, the formulation would be:

```
UPDATE PACKAGE
      SET PACKCOST = PACKCOST * 1.02
      WHERE PACKTYPE = 'Database'
      AND PACKCOST > 400
```

Figure 5.2 shows the results of this command.

Figure 5.2

Cost has been
changed

Before:

PACKAGE

PACKID	PACKNAME	PACKVER	PACKTYPE	PACKCOST
AC01	Boise Accounting	3.00	Accounting	725.83
DB32	Manta	1.50	Database	380.00
DB33	Manta II	2.10	Database	430.18
SS11	Limitless View	5.30	Spreadsheet	217.95
WP08	Words & More	2.00	Word Processing	185.00
WP09	Freeware Processing	4.27	Word Processing	30.00

After:

PACKAGE

PACKID	PACKNAME	PACKVER	PACKTYPE	PACKCOST
AC01	Boise Accounting	3.00	Accounting	725.83
DB32	Manta	1.50	Database	380.00
DB33	Manta II	2.10	Database	438.78
SS11	Limitless View	5.30	Spreadsheet	217.95
WP08	Words & More	2.00	Word Processing	185.00
WP09	Freeware Processing	4.27	Word Processing	30.00

ADDING NEW DATA

You have seen how to do this before. Recall that initially we had to add data to the database in order to load it with data. Here, we use the INSERT command in exactly the same way we did earlier.

Example 49: Add a new employee to the database. The employee number is 402, the name is Robert Sanders (Sanders, Robert), and the phone number is 2056.

To add new data, we use the INSERT command. If we have specific data, as in this example, we can use the insert command as follows:

```
INSERT INTO EMPLOYEE
      VALUES
      (402,'Sanders, Robert',2056)
```

After the word VALUES, we list all the values for the new row. It is essential that these values be listed in the same order as the columns appear in the table. The results of this insertion are shown in Figure 5.3.

Figure 5.3

New employee has been added

Before:

EMPLOYEE

EMPNUM	EMPNAME	EMPPHONE
124	Alvarez, Ramon	1212
567	Feinstein, Betty	8716
611	Dinh, Melissa	2963

After:

EMPLOYEE

EMPNUM	EMPNAME	EMPPHONE
124	Alvarez, Ramon	1212
402	Sanders, Robert	2056
567	Feinstein, Betty	8716
611	Dinh, Melissa	2963

DELETING DATA

Example 50: Delete from the database the employee whose phone number is 8716.

To delete data from the database, use the DELETE command, as in the following:

```
DELETE EMPLOYEE
      WHERE EMPPHONE = 8716
```

Figure 5.4 shows the effect of this deletion on the *EMPLOYEE* table.

Notice that this type of deletion can be dangerous. If there happens to be another employee whose phone number is also 8716, this employee would also be deleted in the process. The safest type of deletion occurs when the condition involves the primary key (for example, deleting employee 567). In such a case, since the primary key is unique, we are certain we will not accidentally delete other rows in the table.

Figure 5.4

Employee has been
deleted

Before:

EMPLOYEE

EMPNUM	EMPNAME	EMPPHONE
124	Alvarez, Ramon	1212
402	Sanders, Robert	2056
567	Feinstein, Betty	8716
611	Dinh, Melissa	2963

After:

EMPLOYEE

EMPNUM	EMPNAME	EMPPHONE
124	Alvarez, Ramon	1212
402	Sanders, Robert	2056
611	Dinh, Melissa	2963

CREATING A NEW TABLE FROM AN EXISTING TABLE

Example 51: Create a new table called *DBPACK* containing the rows in the *PACKAGE* table of type Database.

The first thing to do is to describe this new table using the data definition facilities of SQL, as follows:

```
CREATE TABLE DBPACK
    (PACKID      CHAR(4),
     PACKNAME    CHAR(20),
     PACKVER     DECIMAL(3,2),
     PACKTYPE    CHAR(15),
     PACKCOST    DECIMAL(5,2))
```

Once this is done, we can use the same INSERT command we encountered earlier. Here, however, we use a SELECT command to indicate what is to be inserted into this new table. The exact formulation is:

```
INSERT INTO DBPACK
    SELECT *
        FROM PACKAGE
        WHERE PACKTYPE = 'Database'
```

The new table does not have to have the same columns as the original, nor must the rows be in the same order. Both of these differences are illustrated in Example 52.

Example 52: Create a new table called *WPPACK* containing the package ID, name, and type for all rows in the *PACKAGE* table of type Word Processing. The rows should be sorted by package name.

Again, we first describe this new table:

```
CREATE TABLE DBPACK
    (PACKID      CHAR(4),
     PACKNAME    CHAR(20),
     PACKVER     DECIMAL(3,2),
     PACKCOST    DECIMAL(5,2))
```

Once this is done, we use the following INSERT command:

```
INSERT INTO WPPACK
     SELECT PACKID, PACKNAME, PACKTYPE
     FROM PACKAGE
     WHERE PACKTYPE = 'Word Processing'
     ORDER BY PACKNAME
```

To see the result, we could enter:

```
SELECT *
    FROM WPPACK
```

```
PACKID  PACKNAME            PACKTYPE
WP09    Freeware Processing  Word Processing
WP08    Words & More         Word Processing
```

SETTING A COLUMN TO NULL

There are some special issues involved when dealing with nulls. We have already seen how to add a row in which some of the values were null and how to select rows in which a given column was null. The other thing we must be able to do is to set a column in an existing row to null. This is illustrated in Example 53.

Example 53: Set the phone number of employee 124 to null.

The formulation to make such a change is exactly what it would be for any other value. Simply use the word NULL as the replacement value. The command is:

```
UPDATE EMPLOYEE
    SET EMPPHONE = NULL
    WHERE EMPNUM = 124
```

CHANGING THE DATABASE STRUCTURE

One of the nicest features of a relational DBMS is the ease with which the database structure can be changed. New tables can be added using the CREATE TABLE command you have already seen. Old tables can be removed. Columns can be added or deleted, and their physical characteristics can be changed. In this section, we examine how to accomplish some of these changes.

Alter

In SQL, it is possible to easily alter the structure of an existing table. In contrast, such a change to the structure of existing databases in a nonrelational system is a much more complex process, involving not only changing the description of the structure but using utility programs to unload the data from the current structure and then reload it with the new structure.

Changing a table in SQL is accomplished through the ALTER table command, as the following examples illustrate.

Example 54: Chazy Associates decides to maintain an employee type for each employee in the database. This type is E for executive employees, A for administrative employees, P for professional employees, and H for hourly employees. Add this as a new column in the *EMPLOYEE* table.

To add columns, we use the ADD option of the ALTER command, as follows:

```
ALTER TABLE EMPLOYEE
      ADD EMPTYPE        CHAR(1)
```

The *EMPLOYEE* table now contains an extra column, *EMPTYPE*. Any rows added from this point on will have this extra column. Existing records contain this extra column, effective immediately. The data in any existing row will be changed to reflect the new column the next time the row is updated. However, any time a row is selected for any reason, the system will treat the row as though the column is actually present. Thus, to the user, it will feel as though the structure was changed immediately.

For rows added from this point on, the value of *EMPTYPE* will be assigned as the row is added. For existing rows, some value of *EMPTYPE* must also be assigned. The simplest approach (from the point of view of the DBMS, *not* the user) is to assign the value NULL as an employee type on all existing rows. This requires that *EMPTYPE* accept null values, and some systems actually insist on this. That is, any column added to a table definition *must* accept nulls; the user has no choice in the matter.

A more flexible approach, and one that is supported by some systems, is to allow the user to specify an initial value. In our example, if most employees are of type H, we might set all the employee types for existing employees to H and later change those employees of type E, type A, or type P to the appropriate value. To change the structure and set the value of *EMPTYPE* to H for all existing records, we would type:

```
ALTER TABLE EMPLOYEE
    ADD EMPTYPE       CHAR(1)    INIT = 'H'
```

Notice that if a system will only set new columns to null, we could still accomplish the above initialization by following the ALTER command with an update command:

```
UPDATE EMPLOYEE
    SET EMPTYPE = 'H'
```

While this is not particularly difficult, it still is an extra step. Further, it is desirable for a user to determine whether to allow nulls rather than have the system require them. Thus, it is preferable for the system to support initial values for added columns.

Some systems automatically position newly added columns at the end. Others, however, allow users to determine where to put them. If we want to position *EMPTYPE* before *EMPPHONE*, for example, we could use an ALTER statement such as the following:

```
ALTER TABLE EMPLOYEE
    ADD EMPTYPE       BEFORE EMPPHONE
                      CHAR(1)    INIT = 'H'
```

or, assuming *EMPPHONE* is the third column:

```
ALTER TABLE EMPLOYEE
    ADD EMPTYPE       BEFORE 3
                      CHAR(1)    INIT = 'H'
```

Notice that this column ordering becomes important only when we use a feature such as SELECT * FROM table-name (that is, where the system lists all columns in the order in which they are stored).

Example 55: We no longer need the *PACKVER* column in the *PACKAGE* table, so we should delete it.

We delete a column by using the DELETE option of the ALTER command. In this case, the formulation is:

```
ALTER TABLE PACKAGE
    DELETE PACKVER
```

Example 56: The length of the *EMPNAME* column is too short. Increase it to 30 characters.

We can change characteristics of existing columns by using the CHANGE option of the ALTER command. To change *EMPNAME* so that it now has length 30, the command would be:

```
ALTER TABLE EMPLOYEE
    CHANGE COLUMN EMPNAME TO CHAR(30)
```

Interestingly, many mainframe systems currently do not support this useful type of change while many microcomputer systems do.

Difficult Changes

In some cases, you may wish to make a change to the structure of a database that is beyond the capabilities of your DBMS. Perhaps you need to eliminate a column and your DBMS does not allow this. Maybe you wish to change the column order or combine data from two tables into one. In such situations, all you need to do is to use the CREATE TABLE command to describe the new table. Then insert values into it using the INSERT command combined with an appropriate SELECT statement.

Drop

A table that is no longer needed can be deleted with the DROP command.

Example 57: The *COMPUTER* table is no longer needed in the Chazy Associates database, so we can delete it.

To delete a table, we simply write DROP TABLE, followed by the name of the table. In this case, the command would be:

```
DROP TABLE COMPUTER
```

SUMMARY

Following is a summary of the material covered in Chapter 5:

1. To change existing data in a table, use the UPDATE command.
2. To add new rows to a table, use the INSERT command.
3. To delete rows from a table, use the DELETE command.
4. To create a new table from an existing table, first create the new table using the CREATE command. Then use an INSERT command containing a SELECT command that selects the desired data.
5. To set a given column to null, the clause is "SET column-name = NULL." To test whether a column is null, the clause is "column-name IS NULL."
6. To add a column to a table, use the ALTER TABLE command with the ADD option.

7. To remove a column from a table, use the ALTER TABLE command with the DELETE option.
8. To change the characteristics of a column, use the ALTER TABLE command with the CHANGE option.
9. To delete a table, use the DROP TABLE command.

EXERCISES (CHAZY ASSOCIATES)

Use SQL to make the following changes to the Chazy Associates database. After each change, execute an appropriate query to determine whether the correct change was made.

Note: Before making any changes, make a copy of the Chazy Associates database. That way, after you have made all the changes in these exercises, you can restore the database to its original state by copying this copy over the active version.

1. Change the model for computer M759 to 4GL.
2. Add $10 to the cost of all word processing packages.
3. Add a new PC to the database (tag number: 68464, computer ID: M759, employee number: 611, location: "Home").
4. Delete from the software table all rows on which the package ID is DB32.
5. Describe a new relation to the database called "WPPACK." It contains the package ID, name, version, and cost for all packages whose type is Word Processing. Once this has been done, insert the appropriate data from the *PACKAGE* relation into this new relation.
6. Change the version of package DB32 to null.
7. Add a column called *NUMINST* to the *PACKAGE* table. It is a three-digit number that represents the number of units of the package that have been installed. Set all values of *ALLOC* to zero. Calculate the number of units of package DB32 that are currently installed. Change the value of *NUMINST* for DB32 to this number.
8. Delete the manufacturer's name from the *COMPUTER* table.
9. Increase the length of *PACKNAME* to 30.
10. Remove the *PACKAGE* table from the Chazy Associates database.

EXERCISES (MOVIES)

Use SQL to make the following changes to the Movies database. After each change, execute an appropriate query to determine whether the correct change was made.

Note: Before making any changes, make a copy of the Movies database. That way, after you have made all the changes in these exercises, you can restore the database to its original state by copying this copy over the active version.

1. Change the address of member 4 to 801 College.
2. Add 1 to the number of bonus units for each member who has rented at least 10 units.
3. Add tape 28 (movie number: 20, purchase date: 4/01/91, times rented: 0, member number: null) to the database.
4. Add member 11 (name: Watson, Danielle, address: 292 Harper, city: Grant, state: Mi, number of rentals: 2, bonus: 0, join date: 4/01/91). Change the member numbers on tapes 3 and 28 to 11.
5. Delete all tapes rented by member 2. Delete member 2. (He has run off with our tapes.)
6. Describe a new table to the database called *BIGRNT*. It contains only member number, name, number of rentals, and join date. Once this has been done, insert the member number, name, number of rentals, and join date of all members who have rented more than 10 movies.
7. Change the member number on tape 4 to null.
8. Add a column called *DUEBACK* to the *TAPE* table. The column will contain the date when each tape is due to be returned. Initially, all values of *DUEBACK* should be null. Change the value of *DUEBACK* for tape 5 to 4/15/91.
9. The club is no longer offering any bonus units. Delete the *BONUS* column from the *MEMBER* table.
10. Increase the length of *MMBNAME* to 30.
11. Remove the *TAPE* table from the Movies database.

Database Administration

OBJECTIVES

When you have completed this chapter, you should understand the following:

1. How views give users their own pictures of the database.
2. The advantages of using views as well as some of the problems.
3. How to use the GRANT mechanism to provide security.
4. How to create an index.
5. The purpose, advantages, and disadvantages of using an index.
6. The structure of the SQL catalog.
7. How to obtain information concerning the structure of a database from the SQL catalog.
8. The support SQL provides for integrity through the Integrity Enhancement Feature (IEF).

INTRODUCTION

There are some special issues involved in managing a database. This process, often called **database administration**, is especially important when the database might be used by more than one person. In a business organization, a person or even a whole group is charged with this function.

We will now investigate some of the features that would be used in database administration. One function of the database administrator, changing the structure of a database, was covered in Chapter 5. In this chapter, we will examine how each user can be given his or her own view of the database. We will see how the GRANT command can be used to give different privileges to different users. We will discuss how indexes can be used to improve performance. Finally, we will see how SQL keeps information about the structure of the database in a special place called the catalog. The database administrator can easily obtain useful information concerning the database structure from the catalog. The database administrator can also specify integrity constraints, that is, rules that the data in the database must satisfy.

VIEWS

A good DBMS can give each user his or her own picture of the database. In SQL, this is done through views. The existing, permanent tables in a relational database are often called **base tables**. A **view** is a pseudotable, which means that it appears to the user to be an actual table. The data doesn't really exist in this fashion, however. Rather, SQL will derive its contents from data in existing base tables whenever users attempt to access the view. The manner in which this data is to be derived is stored as part of the view definition.

Defining and Using Views

A view is defined through a **defining query** as illustrated in Example 58.

Example 58: Define a view, *DATABASE*, that consists of the package ID, the package name, and the cost of all packages whose type is Database.

This would be accomplished as follows:

```
CREATE VIEW DATABASE AS
      SELECT PACKID, PACKNAME, PACKCOST
          FROM PACKAGE
          WHERE PACKTYPE = 'Database'
```

Given the current data in the database, this view will contain the data shown in Figure 6.1. The data does not actually exist in this form, however, nor will it *ever* exist in this form. It is tempting to think that when this view is used, the query will be executed and will produce some sort of temporary table, called *DATABASE*, which the user will then access. This is *not* what happens. Instead, the query acts as a sort of "window" into the database (see Figure 6.2). As far as a user of this view is concerned, the whole database consists of the dark portion of the *PACKAGE* table.

Figure 6.1

DATABASE view

DATABASE

PACKID	PACKNAME	PACKCOST
DB32	Manta	380.00
DB33	Manta	430.18

This is implemented cleverly. Suppose, for example, a user of this view typed the following query:

Figure 6.2

Chazy Associates
sample data

PACKAGE

PACKID	PACKNAME	PACKVER	PACKTYPE	PACKCOST
AC01	Boise Accounting	3.00	Accounting	725.83
DB32	Manta	1.50	Database	380.00
DB33	Manta	2.10	Database	430.18
SS11	Limitless View	5.30	Spreadsheet	217.95
WP08	Words & More	2.00	Word Processing	185.00
WP09	Freeware Processing	4.27	Word Processing	30.00

```
SELECT *
    FROM DATABASE
    WHERE PACKCOST > 400
```

Rather than being executed directly, this query is first merged with the query that defines the view, producing:

```
SELECT PACKID, PACKNAME, PACKCOST
    FROM PACKAGE
    WHERE PACKTYPE = 'Database'
    AND PACKCOST > 400
```

Notice that the selection is from the *PACKAGE* table, rather than the *DATABASE* view; the "***" is replaced by just those columns in the *DATABASE* view; and the condition involves the condition in the query entered by the user, together with the condition stated in the view definition. This new query is the one that is actually executed.

The user, however, is unaware that this kind of activity is taking place. It seems there actually is a table called *DATABASE* being accessed. One advantage of this approach is that since *DATABASE* never exists in its own right, any update to the *PACKAGE* table is *immediately* felt by someone accessing the database through the *DATABASE* view. If *DATABASE* were an actual stored table, this would not be the case.

The form of a view definition is illustrated in the *DATABASE* view. It is CREATE view-name AS query. The query, which is called the **defining query**, can be any legitimate SQL query. (This is not technically true for all relational model implementations. Some forbid the use of UNION in the query, for example.) Optionally, the view-name can be followed by the names for columns in the view, as:

```
CREATE VIEW DATABASE (PACKID, PACKNAME, PACKCOST) AS
    SELECT PACKID, PACKNAME, PACKCOST
        FROM PACKAGE
        WHERE PACKTYPE = 'Database'
```

This feature can also be used to rename columns, as Example 59 shows.

Example 59: Define a view, *DATABASE*, that consists of the package ID, the package name, and the cost of all packages whose type is Database. In this view, the package ID column is to be called *PKID*, the package name column is to be called *NAME*, and the package cost column is to be called *COST*.

We simply include the desired column names in parentheses, as follows:

```
CREATE VIEW DATABASE (PKID, NAME, COST) AS
    SELECT PACKID, PACKNAME, PACKCOST
        FROM PACKAGE
        WHERE PACKTYPE = 'Database'
```

In this case, anyone accessing the *DATABASE* view will refer to *PACKID* as *PKID*, *PACKNAME* as *NAME*, and *PACKCOST* as *COST*.

The *DATABASE* view is an example of a row-and-column subset view, that is, it consists of a subset of the rows and columns in some base table (in this case, the *PACKAGE* table). Since the query can be any SQL query, a view could involve the join of two or more tables. It could also involve statistics. Example 60 involves a join.

Example 60: Define a view, *PCEMP*, that consists of the tag number, computer ID, employee number, and employee name for all PCs and matching employees in the *PC* and *EMPLOYEE* tables.

The command to create this view would be:

```
CREATE VIEW PCEMP AS
    SELECT TAGNUM, COMPID, PC.EMPNUM, EMPNAME
        FROM PC, EMPLOYEE
        WHERE PC.EMPNUM = EMPLOYEE.EMPNUM
```

Given the current data, this view is the table shown in Figure 6.3. Example 61 is a view that involves statistics.

Figure 6.3

PCEMP view

PCEMP

TAGNUM	COMPID	EMPNUM	EMPNAME
32808	M759	611	Dinh, Melissa
37691	B121	124	Alvarez, Ramon
57772	C007	567	Feinstein, Betty
59836	B221	124	Alvarez, Ramon
77740	M759	567	Feinstein, Betty

Example 61: Define a view, *TYPEPACK*, that consists of a package type and the number of packages (*NUMBPACK*) that are of that type.

To create this view, we would use the following command:

```
CREATE VIEW TYPEPACK (PACKTYPE, NUMBPACK) AS
     SELECT PACKTYPE, COUNT(PACKID)
          FROM PACKAGE
          GROUP BY PACKTYPE
```

Given the current data, this view is the table shown in Figure 6.4.

Figure 6.4

TYPEPACK view

TYPEPACK

PACKTYPE	NUMBPACK
Accounting	1
Database	2
Spreadsheet	1
Word Processing	2

Advantages of Views

The use of views furnishes several advantages:

1. Views provide data independence. If the database structure is changed (columns added, relationships changed, and so forth.) in such a way that the view can still be derived from existing data, the user can still access the same view. If adding extra columns to tables in the database is the only change and these columns are not required by this user, the defining query may not even need to be changed. If relationships are changed, the defining query may be different. But since users need not even be aware of the defining query, this difference is unknown to them. They continue to access the database through the same view, as though nothing has changed.
2. Since each user has his or her own view, the same data can be viewed by different users in different ways.
3. A view should contain only those columns required by a given user. This practice accomplishes two things. First, since the view will likely contain far fewer columns than the overall database and since the view is effectively a single table, rather than a collection of tables, it greatly simplifies the user's perception of the database. Second, it furnishes a measure of security. Columns that are not included in the view are not accessible to this user. In a view built on a faculty table, for example, omitting the *SALARY* column from the view will ensure that a user of this view cannot access any faculty member's salary. Likewise, rows that are not included in the view are not accessible. A *DATABASE* view user, for example, cannot obtain any information about packages of other types.

The above advantages hold when views are used for retrieval purposes only; the story is a little different when it comes to updates. The issues involved in updating data through a view depend on the type of view.

Row and Column Subsets.   Consider the row and column subset view *DATA-BASE*. There are columns in the underlying base table, *PACKAGE*, that are not present in the view. Thus, if we attempt to add a row ('FH54','FASTDB',350.00), somehow the system must determine how to fill in values for the remaining columns: *PACKVER* and *PACKTYPE*. In this case, it is clear how to fill in *PACK-TYPE*. According to the definition of the view, it should be Database.

It is not at all clear how to fill in *PACKVER*, however. The only possibility would be NULL. Thus, provided that any columns not included in a view may accept nulls, we can add new rows in the fashion previously indicated.

There is another problem. Suppose the user attempts to add the row ('AC01','DATAQUICK',250.00). This attempt *must* be rejected, since there is already a package with AC01 as the ID in the *PACKAGE* table. This rejection will certainly seem strange to the user, since there is no such package in this user's view! (It has a different type.)

Updates or deletions cause no particular problem in this view. If the description of package DB33 is changed from Manta to Manta II, this change will be made in the *PACKAGE* table. If package DB32 is deleted, this deletion will occur in the *PACKAGE* table.

While some problems do have to be overcome, it seems possible to update the database through the *DATABASE* view. This does not imply that *any* row and column subset view is updatable, however. Consider the following view:

```
CREATE VIEW VERCOST AS
      SELECT PACKVER, PACKCOST
          FROM PACKAGE
```

How would we add the row (3.1, 225.00) to this view? In the underlying base table, *PACKAGE*, we would need to add a package with this version and this cost. We can't leave the other columns null in this case, especially since one of them is *PACKID*, which is the primary key. In general, a row and column subset view that contains the primary key of the underlying base table is updatable (provided, of course, the missing columns allow null as a possible value).

Joins.   In general, views that involve joins of base tables can cause real problems at update. Consider the relatively simple view *PCEMP*, for example, described earlier. (See Figure 6.3.) The fact that some columns in the underlying base tables are not seen in this view certainly presents some of the same problems discussed earlier. Even assuming that these problems can be overcome through the use of nulls, there are more serious problems inherent in the attempt to update the database through this view. On the surface, changing the name Ramon Alvarez on the second row to Ramon Sanchez might not appear to pose any problems other than some inconsistency in the data. (In the new version of the row, the name of employee 124 is Ramon Sanchez; on the fourth row in the table, the name of employee 124 is still Ramon Alvarez.) The problem is actually more serious than that because it is not possible to make only this change! Since the name of the employee is stored just once in the underlying employee table, changing the name to Ramon Alvarez on this one row of the view will cause the same change to be made on all the other rows. Although in this case that would probably be a good thing, in general, unexpected changes caused by an update are definitely *not* desirable.

Before leaving the topic of views that involve joins, note that not all joins create the preceding problem. If two base tables happen to have the same primary key and this primary key is used as the join field, updating the database will not be a problem. For example, what if the actual database contains not a single *PACKAGE* table but two (Figure 6.5):

        PACKDESC(PACKID, PACKNAME, PACKTYPE)

and

        PACKCOST(PACKID, PACKVER, PACKCOST)

Figure 6.5

Package data split across two relations

PACKDESC

PACKID	PACKNAME	PACKTYPE
AC01	Boise Accounting	Accounting
DB32	Manta	Database
DB33	Manta	Database
SS11	Limitless View	Spreadsheet
WP08	Words & More	Word Processing
WP09	Freeware Processing	Word Processing

PACKCOST

PACKID	PACKVER	PACKCOST
AC01	3.00	725.83
DB32	1.50	380.00
DB33	2.10	430.18
SS11	5.30	217.95
WP08	2.00	185.00
WP09	4.27	30.00

In this case, what was a single table in the original database has been divided into two. Any user who expected to see a single table could be accommodated through a view that joined these two tables together on *PACKID*. We could, in fact, call the view *PACKAGE*. The view definition would be:

```
CREATE VIEW PACKAGE AS
        SELECT PACKDESC.PACKID, PACKNAME, PACKVER, PACKTYPE,
                PACKCOST
        FROM PACKDESC, PACKCOST
        WHERE PACKDESC.PACKID = PACKCOST.PACKID
```

This view would contain the data shown in Figure 6.6.

Figure 6.6

PACKAGE as a view that is a join of *PACKDESC* and *PACKCOST*

PACKAGE

PACKID	PACKNAME	PACKVER	PACKTYPE	PACKCOST
AC01	Boise Accounting	3.00	Accounting	725.83
DB32	Manta	1.50	Database	380.00
DB33	Manta	2.10	Database	430.18
SS11	Limitless View	5.30	Spreadsheet	217.95
WP08	Words & More	2.00	Word Processing	185.00
WP09	Freeware Processing	4.27	Word Processing	30.00

There is no difficulty encountered in updating this view. Adding a row simply involves adding a row to each of the underlying base tables. A change to any row in the view requires only a change to the appropriate base table. To delete any row from the view, we delete the corresponding rows from both underlying base tables.

Question: How would you add the row (SS57, Quickview, 1.0, Spreadsheet, 159.95)?

Answer: Add the row (SS57, Quickview, Spreadsheet) to *PACKDESC* and the row (SS57, 1.0, 159.95) to *PACKCOST*.

Question: How would you change the name of package DB33 to Manta II?

Answer: Change the name in *PACKDESC*.

Q & A

Question:	How would you change the cost of package DB33 to 410.00?
Answer:	Make the change in *PACKCOST*.

Q & A

Question:	How would you delete package DB32?
Answer:	Delete the package from *both PACKDESC and PACKCOST*.

The previously discussed view *PACKAGE* is updatable. None of the types of updates (add, change, or delete) causes any problems. The main reason that this view is updatable and other views involving joins are not is that this view is derived from the joining of two base tables *on the primary key of each*. In contrast, the view *PCEMP* is derived from joining two tables using the primary key of one table and a matching foreign primary key in the other. Even more severe problems are encountered if neither of the columns used in the join is a primary key.

Statistics. A view that involves statistics calculated from one or more base tables is the most troublesome of all. Consider *TYPEPACK*, for example. (See Figure 6.4.) How would we add the row (Graphics, 4)? We would somehow have to add to the database four packages, each of whose type is Graphics. Likewise, changing the row (Accounting, 1) to (Accounting, 4) means adding three packages, each of whose type is Accounting. These are clearly impossible tasks.

Current Systems

The preceding discussion concerned what is *theoretically possible*, not what is actually implemented on current commercial systems. Many current systems support update of views that are row and column subsets. (In performing this kind of update, keep in mind some of the pitfalls we've discussed.) Views involving statistics are not even *theoretically* updatable. Views involving joins form the middle ground. Some such views are not theoretically updatable, whereas others are. Many current implementations will not support update of the database through any view that involves a join, even views that are updatable in theory. Some systems are beginning to support some type of update of join views, however. We will certainly see more of this in the next few years.

Dropping a View

When a view is no longer needed, it can be removed by using the DROP VIEW command.

Example 62: The *DATABASE* view is no longer necessary, so we remove it.

This is done with the DROP VIEW command:

```
DROP VIEW DATABASE
```

SECURITY

Security is the prevention of unauthorized access to the database. Within an organization, some person or group will determine the types of access various users can have to the database. Some users might be able to retrieve and update anything in the database. Other users may be able to retrieve any data from the database but not make any changes to the data. Still other users may only be able to access a portion of the database. For example, Bill may be able to retrieve and update employee data but not retrieve data about PCs and software packages. Mary may be able to retrieve data on software packages and nothing else. Sam may be able to retrieve and update data on database packages, but no others.

Once these rules have been determined, it's up to the DBMS to enforce them. In particular, it's up to whatever security mechanism the DBMS provides. In SQL systems, there are two security mechanisms. We have already seen that views furnish a certain amount of security. (If someone is accessing the database through a view, that person cannot access any data that is not part of the view.) The main mechanism, however, is the GRANT facility. The basic idea is that different types of privileges can be granted to users and, if necessary, later revoked. These privileges include such things as the right to select rows from a table, the right to insert new rows, the right to update existing rows, and so on. Granting and revoking these privileges is accomplished through GRANT and REVOKE statements. Following are some examples of the GRANT statement.

Example 63: User Jones must be able to retrieve data from the *EMPLOYEE* table.

```
GRANT SELECT ON EMPLOYEE TO JONES
```

Example 64: Users Smith and Brown must be able to add new packages.

```
GRANT INSERT ON PACKAGE TO SMITH, BROWN
```

Example 65: User Anderson must be able to change the name or phone number of employees.

```
GRANT UPDATE ON EMPLOYEE (EMPNAME, EMPPHONE) TO ANDERSON
```

Example 66: User Martin must be able to delete software records.

```
GRANT DELETE ON SOFTWARE TO MARTIN
```

Example 67: All users must be able to retrieve package IDs, names, and types.

```
GRANT SELECT ON PACKAGE (PACKID, PACKNAME, PACKTYPE)
      TO PUBLIC
```

Example 68: User Roberts must be able to create an index on the *COMPUTER* table.

(*Note:* Indexes and their use will be discussed in the next section. This example merely covers granting a user the privilege to create an index.)

```
GRANT INDEX ON COMPUTER TO ROBERTS
```

Example 69: User Thomas must be able to change the structure of the *EMPLOYEE* table.

```
GRANT ALTER ON EMPLOYEE TO THOMAS
```

Example 70: User Wilson must have all privileges on the *COMPUTER*, *EMPLOYEE*, and *PC* tables.

```
GRANT ALL ON COMPUTER, EMPLOYEE, PC TO WILSON
```

The privileges that can be granted are SELECT (retrieve data), UPDATE (change data), DELETE (delete data), INSERT (add new data), ALTER (change the structure of a table), and INDEX (create an index). Any GRANT statement can be followed with the clause WITH GRANT OPTION, which will allow the user mentioned in the GRANT statement not only the appropriate privileges but also the ability to GRANT these same privileges (or a subset of them) to still other users.

Any privileges granted in this fashion can later be revoked by using the REVOKE statement. The format of the REVOKE statement is essentially the same as that of the GRANT statement, but there are two differences. Instead of GRANT privileges TO users, the format is REVOKE privileges FROM users. In addition, the clause WITH GRANT OPTION is obviously not meaningful as part of a REVOKE statement. Incidentally, the revoke will "cascade"; that is, if Jones was granted privileges WITH GRANT OPTION and then Jones granted these same privileges to Smith, revoking the privileges from Jones will revoke Smith's privileges at the same time. Example 71 illustrates the use of the REVOKE command.

Example 71: User Jones is no longer allowed to retrieve data from the *EMPLOYEE* table.

```
REVOKE SELECT ON EMPLOYEE FROM JONES
```

GRANT and REVOKE can also be applied to views. This provides the capability of restricting access only to certain rows within tables.

Example 72: Permit Marilyn Johnson, the database specialist at Chazy Associates, to access any data concerning packages of type Database, but do not allow her to access data concerning any other packages.

This could be accomplished as follows:

```
CREATE VIEW DBPACK AS
      SELECT *
            FROM PACKAGE
            WHERE PACKID = 'Database'
GRANT SELECT ON DBPACK TO MARILYN JOHNSON
```

INDEXES

Purpose of an Index

Much of what we do when we manipulate a database involves finding a row or collection of rows that satisfies some condition. Examining every single row in a table looking for the desired rows often takes far too long to be practical. Fortunately, there is an alternative approach that can greatly speed up the process. This approach involves the use of what is called an **index**. You are probably already familiar with this idea. If you wanted to find a discussion of a given topic in a book, you could scan the entire book from start to finish, looking for references to the topic you had in mind. More than likely, however, you wouldn't have to resort to this technique. If the book had a good *index*, you would use it to rapidly locate the pages on which your topic was discussed.

Within relational model systems on both mainframes and microcomputers, the main mechanism for increasing the efficiency with which data is retrieved from the database is the use of indexes. These indexes are very much like the index in a book. Consider Figure 6.7, for example, which shows the *PC* table

Figure 6.7

PC table with record numbers

PC

REC	TAGNUM	COMPID	EMPNUM	LOCATION
1	32808	M759	611	Accounting
2	37691	B121	124	Sales
3	57772	C007	567	Info Systems
4	59836	B221	124	Home
5	77740	M759	567	Home

together with one extra column, *REC*. This extra column gives the number of each record within the file. (PC 32808 is on record 1; PC 37691 is on record 2; and so on.) These record numbers are used by the DBMS to allow it to go directly to a specific row. They are not used by the users of the DBMS, and that is why we do not normally show them. Here, however, we are dealing with the manner in which the DBMS works, so we do need to be aware of them.

In order to rapidly access a PC on the basis of its tag number, we might choose to create and use an index as shown in Figure 6.8. The index is a separate file that has two columns. The first column contains a tag number, and the second column includes the number of the record on which the PC with that tag number is found. To find a PC, we look up the PC's tag number in the first column in the index. The value in the second column indicates which record we should retrieve from the *PC* table. We proceed directly to the desired record, and we have the PC we want.

Figure 6.8

Index for *PC* table on *TAGNUM* column

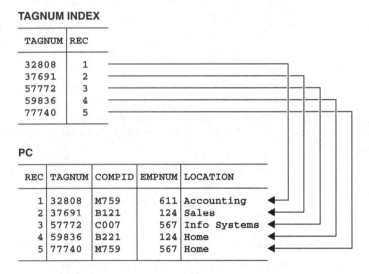

Since tag numbers are unique, there will be a single record number in each row in the index. This need not always be the case, however. Suppose we wanted to be able to rapidly access all PCs with a particular computer ID. Consider that we would also like to be able to rapidly access all PCs assigned to a given employee. In this case, we might choose to create and use an index on computer ID, as well as an index on employee number. (See Figure 6.9.) In the index on computer ID, the first column contains a computer ID and the second column contains the numbers of *all* the records on which that ID is found. The index on employee number is similar, except that the first column contains an employee number.

Figure 6.9

Indexes for *PC*
table on *COMPID*
and *EMPNUM*
columns

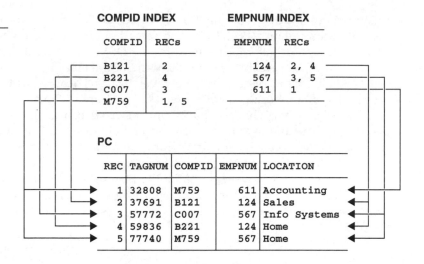

Question: How would you find all PCs whose computer ID is M759?

Answer: Look up M759 in the *COMPID* index. This will give you a collection of record numbers (1 and 5). Use these record numbers to find the corresponding PCs (32808 and 77740).

Question: How would you find all PCs assigned to employee 567?

Answer: Look up 567 in the *EMPNUM* index. This will give you a collection of record numbers (3 and 5). Use these record numbers to find the corresponding PCs (57772 and 77740).

There is another potential use for indexes. If we follow the record numbers in the order they are listed, the data appears to be sorted by the field on which the index was built. If we use the *COMPID* index, for example, we would first list record 2, then record 4, then record 3, and finally records 1 and 5. This would produce the following output:

```
TAGNUM    COMPID    EMPNUM    LOCATION
37691     B121         124    Sales
59836     B221         124    Home
57772     C007         567    Info Systems
32808     M759         611    Accounting
77740     M759         567    Home
```

The data appears to be sorted by computer ID. If, on the other hand, we use the *EMPNUM* index, we would list the records in a different order. We would list record 2, then record 4, then record 3, then record 5, and lastly, record 1. This time, the output appears to be sorted by employee number:

```
TAGNUM    COMPID    EMPNUM    LOCATION
37691     B121         124    Sales
59836     B221         124    Home
57772     C007         567    Info Systems
77740     M759         567    Home
32808     M759         611    Accounting
```

Using an existing index to order the output in this fashion is usually much more efficient than actually sorting the data in the database.

The actual structure of these indexes is a bit more complicated than what we have been looking at here, although what we have seen is fine for our purposes. (Indexes typically use the B-tree structure. If you are interested in information on B-trees, consult any book on data structures.)

Fortunately, we don't have to be concerned with the details of manipulating and using these indexes. The DBMS will do all this for us. We merely decide which columns indexes should be built on. Typically, an index can be created and maintained for any column or combination of columns in any table. Once an index exists, the DBMS can use it to facilitate retrieval. In powerful relational systems, the decision concerning which index or indexes to use (if any) during a particular type of retrieval is one function of a part of the DBMS called an **optimizer**. (No reference is made to any index by the user; rather, the system makes the decision behind the scenes.)

As you would expect, the use of any index is not purely advantageous or disadvantageous. The advantages were already mentioned: an index makes certain types of retrieval more efficient and an index can be an efficient alternative to sorting. There are two disadvantages. First, an index occupies space that could be used for something else. Any retrieval that can be made using an index can also be made without the index. The process may be less efficient, but it is still possible. So an index, while it occupies space, is technically unnecessary. Second, the index must be updated whenever corresponding data in the database is updated. Without the index, these updates would not have to be performed. The main question to ask when considering whether to create an index is: Do the benefits derived during retrieval outweigh the additional storage required and the extra processing involved in update operations?

You can add or drop indexes at will. Furthermore, you do not have to make the final decision concerning the columns or combination of columns on which indexes should be built at the time the database is first implemented. If the pattern of access to the database later indicates that overall performance would benefit from the creation of a new index, you can easily add it. Likewise, if an existing index proves unnecessary, it can easily be dropped.

Creating and Dropping Indexes

The commands used to create an index are CREATE INDEX and CREATE UNIQUE INDEX. Following are examples of the use of these commands for creating indexes for the Chazy Associates database.

Example 73: Create a unique index on the *PACKID* column within the *PACKAGE* table. The index is to be called *PACKIND*.

The word UNIQUE indicates that the system is to maintain uniqueness of package IDs (that is, the system will not permit two packages with the same ID to exist in the database). This index will be used to support direct retrieval based on the primary key, *PACKID*.) The command to create this index is:

```
CREATE UNIQUE INDEX PACKIND ON PACKAGE (PACKID)
```

Example 74: Create an index called *CUSTIND2* on the *COMPID* column within the *EMPLOYEE* table.

```
CREATE INDEX CUSTIND2 ON EMPLOYEE (COMPID)
```

Example 75: Create a unique index called *SOFTIND* on the *PACKID, TAGNUM* combination, which is the primary key of the *SOFTWARE* table.

To create an index on more than one field, simply list all the fields, as in:

```
CREATE UNIQUE INDEX SOFTIND
          ON SOFTWARE (PACKID, TAGNUM)
```

Example 76: Create an index for the *PACKAGE* table, called *PACKIND3* on the combination of package name and descending package version (that is, the latest version will be listed first).

If packages are listed using this index, they will appear in order of package name. Within any group of packages with the same name, the packages will be ordered by version number in reverse order. The only thing new about this example is the fact that the version number is to be in descending order. To accomplish this, simply follow *PACKVER* with DESC, as in the following:

```
CREATE INDEX PACKIND3 ON PACKAGE (PACKNAME, PACKVER DESC)
```

Dropping an Index

The command used to drop an index is DROP INDEX.

Example 77: Delete the index called *PACKIND*.

The command is:

```
DROP INDEX PACKIND
```

Index Discussion

These indexes are very efficient and, if a given type of retrieval will be performed with any frequency, an index to facilitate the process is usually worthwhile. In such situations, the added efficiency, will usually offset the additional storage required and the extra overhead in processing incurred when updating the database. The ability to create and drop indexes easily, together with an efficient optimizer, provides a great deal of flexibility. If an index were created on a given date that would increase the efficiency of a given type of retrieval, the optimizer should immediately begin making use of the index. There is no need for a program change. The only difference a user might notice is that certain types of retrieval would be more rapid and certain types of updates might be less rapid. Likewise, if an index were dropped on a particular date, the optimizer would find new ways of satisfying any request that utilized that index. Again, there is no need for a program change. In this case, the only apparent difference might be that certain types of retrieval would be less rapid and certain types of update might be more rapid. The flexibility to make this type of change "on the fly" is one of the real benefits of the relational model systems that is not shared by systems following other models.

THE CATALOG

Information about the tables known to the system is kept in the system **catalog**. In the following description of the catalog, the exact structure has been somewhat oversimplified, but it represents the basic ideas.

The catalog contains several tables of its own. We will focus on three of the most important: *SYSTABLES* (information about the tables known to SQL), *SYSCOLUMNS* (information about the columns within these tables), and *SYSINDEXES* (information about indexes defined on these tables.) While these tables have many columns, only a few are of concern to us here.

SYSTABLES (see Figure 6.10) contains columns *NAME*, *CREATOR*, and *COLCOUNT*. The *NAME* column identifies the name of a table. The *CREATOR* column contains an identification of the person or group who created the table. The *COLCOUNT* column contains the number of columns within the table being described. If, for example, user Brown created the *EMPLOYEE* table and the *EMPLOYEE* table has three columns, there is a row in the *SYSTABLES* table in which *NAME* is EMPLOYEE, *CREATOR* is BROWN, and *COLCOUNT* is 3. Similar rows would exist for all tables known to the system.

Figure 6.10

SYSTABLES table

SYSTABLES

NAME	CREATOR	COLCOUNT
COMPUTER	BROWN	4
EMPLOYEE	BROWN	3
PC	BROWN	4
PACKAGE	BROWN	5
SOFTWARE	BROWN	4

SYSCOLUMNS (see Figure 6.11) contains columns *COLNAME, TBNAME,* and *COLTYPE.* The *COLNAME* column identifies the name of a column in one of the tables. The table in which the column is found is stored in *TBNAME,* and the data type for the column is found in *COLTYPE.* For example, there is a row in *SYSCOLUMNS* for each column in the *EMPLOYEE* table. On each of these rows, *TBNAME* is EMPLOYEE. On one of these rows, *COLNAME* is EMPNUM and *COLTYPE* is DECIMAL (3). On another row, *COLNAME* is EMPNAME and *COL-TYPE* is CHAR(20). Similar rows exist for all columns known to the system.

Figure 6.11

SYSCOLUMNS table

SYSCOLUMNS

COLNAME	TBNAME	COLTYPE
COMPID	COMPUTER	CHAR(4)
MFGNAME	COMPUTER	CHAR(6)
MFGMODEL	COMPUTER	CHAR(3)
PROCTYPE	COMPUTER	CHAR(6)
EMPNUM	EMPLOYEE	DECIMAL(3)
EMPNAME	EMPLOYEE	CHAR(20)
EMPPHONE	EMPLOYEE	DECIMAL(4)
TAGNUM	PC	CHAR(5)
COMPID	PC	CHAR(4)
EMPNUM	PC	DECIMAL(3)
LOCATION	PC	CHAR(12)
PACKID	PACKAGE	CHAR(4)
PACKNAME	PACKAGE	CHAR(20)
PACKVER	PACKAGE	DECIMAL(4,2)
PACKTYPE	PACKAGE	CHAR(15)
PACKCOST	PACKAGE	DECIMAL(6,2)
PACKID	SOFTWARE	CHAR(4)
TAGNUM	SOFTWARE	CHAR(5)
INSTDATE	SOFTWARE	DATE
SOFTCOST	SOFTWARE	DECIMAL(6,2)

SYSINDEXES contains columns *NAME, TBNAME,* and *CREATOR.* The name of the index is found in the *NAME* column. The name of the table on which the index was built is found in the *TBNAME* column. The ID of the person or group that created the index is found in the *CREATOR* column.

The system catalog is a relational database of its own. Consequently, the same types of queries used to retrieve information from relational databases generally can be used to retrieve information from the system catalog. The following examples illustrate this process.

Example 78: List the name and creator of all tables known to the system.

```
SELECT NAME, CREATOR
    FROM SYSTABLES
```

Example 79: List all the columns in the *PACKAGE* table as well as their associated data types.

```
SELECT COLNAME, COLTYPE
    FROM SYSCOLUMNS
    WHERE TBNAME = 'PACKAGE'
```

Example 80: List all tables that contain a column called *EMPNUM*.

```
SELECT TBNAME
    FROM SYSCOLUMNS
    WHERE COLNAME = 'EMPNUM'
```

Thus, information concerning the tables in our relational database, the columns they contain, and the indexes built on them can be obtained from the catalog by using the same SQL syntax used to query any other relational database.

Updating the tables that constitute the catalog occurs automatically when users CREATE, ALTER, or DROP tables or when they CREATE or DROP indexes. Users should not update the catalog directly using the update features of SQL because inconsistent results may be produced. Suppose, for example, a user were to delete the row in the *SYSCOLUMNS* table for the *PACKID* column within the *PACKAGE* table. The system would no longer have any knowledge of this column, which is the primary key, yet all the rows in the *PACKAGE* table would still contain a package ID. The system might now treat those IDs as package names, since, as far as it is concerned, *PACKNAME* is the first column in the *PACKAGE* table.

INTEGRITY IN SQL

The original standard approved by **ANSI** (the American National Standards Institute) did not contain any provisions for integrity support. An additional component, called the **IEF** (Integrity Enhancement Feature), was added later. This is the component that furnishes support for integrity. Many existing versions of SQL have not yet added this support, although this will undoubtedly come soon.

The IEF furnishes three types of integrity support:

Legal values. The CHECK clause is now available to ensure that only values that satisfy a particular condition are allowed in a given column. For example, to ensure that the only legal values for locations are "Accounting," "Sales," "Info Systems," and "Home," the clause would be:

```
CHECK (PC.LOCATION IN ('Accounting', 'Sales', 'Info Systems',
    'Home') )
```

or, equivalently,

```
CHECK (PC.LOCATION = 'Accounting' OR PC.LOCATION = 'Sales'
    OR PC.LOCATION = 'Info Systems' OR PC.LOCATION = 'Home')
```

The general form of the CHECK clause is simply the word CHECK followed by a condition. If any update to the database would result in the condition being violated, the update will automatically be rejected.

Primary keys. The primary key for a table is specified through the PRIMARY KEY clause. For example, to indicate that *TAGNUM* is the primary key for the *PC* table, the clause would be:

```
PRIMARY KEY (TAGNUM)
```

In general, the PRIMARY KEY clause has the form PRIMARY KEY followed by the column, or columns, that make up the primary key in parentheses. If more than one column is included, the columns are separated by commas. Thus, the primary key clause for the *SOFTWARE* table would be

```
PRIMARY KEY (PACKID, TAGNUM)
```

Foreign keys. Any foreign keys are specified through FOREIGN KEY clauses. To specify a foreign key, we need to specify *both* the column that is a foreign key *and* the table it is to match. In the *PC* table, for example, *COMPID* is a foreign key that must match the *COMPUTER* table. This is specified as:

```
FOREIGN KEY (COMPID) REFERENCES COMPUTER
```

The general form is FOREIGN KEY, followed first by the column, or columns, that constitute the foreign key, then the word REFERENCES, and, finally, by the name of the table the foreign key is supposed to match.

Example 81: Create the *PC* table for the Chazy Associates database. Valid locations are to be 'Accounting,' 'Sales,' 'Info Systems,' and 'Home'. The primary key is to be *TAGNUM*. *COMPID* is a foreign key that is required to match the primary key of the *COMPUTER* table, and *EMPNUM* is a foreign key that is required to match the primary key of the *EMPLOYEE* table.

We have already discussed all the components of the necessary CREATE TABLE statement. The full statement is:

```
CREATE TABLE PC
     ( TAGNUM       CHAR(5),
       COMPID       CHAR(4),
       EMPNUM       DECIMAL(3),
       LOCATION     CHAR(12)
       CHECK (PC.LOCATION IN ('Accounting', 'Sales',
             'Info Systems', 'Home') )
       PRIMARY KEY (TAGNUM)
       FOREIGN KEY (COMPID) REFERENCES COMPUTER
       FOREIGN KEY (EMPNUM) REFERENCES EMPLOYEE )
```

SUMMARY

Following is a summary of the material covered in Chapter 6:

1. A view is a pseudotable whose contents are derived from data in existing base tables whenever users attempt to access the view.
2. To define a view, use the CREATE VIEW statement. This statement includes a defining query that describes the portion of the database included in the view. When a user retrieves data from the view, the query entered by the user is merged with the defining query, producing the query that SQL will actually execute.
3. Views provide data independence, allow different users to view data in the database in different ways, and simplify things for users. Some views, however, cannot be used for update purposes.
4. To give users access privileges concerning various portions of the database, use the GRANT command.
5. To terminate previously granted privileges, use the REVOKE command.
6. Indexes can be used to make retrieval much more efficient.
7. To create an index, use the CREATE INDEX command.
8. To delete an index, use the DROP INDEX command.
9. SQL, not the user, decides which index to use to accomplish a given task.
10. Information about the tables, columns, indexes, and so on is kept in the system catalog. Information about tables is kept in a special table called *SYSTABLES*; information about columns is kept in *SYSCOLUMNS*; and information about indexes is kept in *SYSINDEXES*.
11. To obtain information from the catalog, use the SELECT command. Users do not update the catalog; the DBMS is responsible for this.
12. To specify a general integrity constraint, use the CHECK clause. To specify a

primary key, use the PRIMARY KEY clause. To specify a foreign key, use the FOREIGN KEY clause. All of these clauses are part of the Integrity Enhancement Feature (IEF) of SQL.

EXERCISES (Chazy Associates)

1. A view, *SMLLPACK*, is to be defined. It consists of the package ID, name, type, and cost for each package whose cost is $400 or less.
   a. Write the view definition for *SMLLPACK*.
   b. Write an SQL query to retrieve the ID and name of all packages in *SMLLPACK* whose type is Database.
   c. Convert the query from part b to the query that will actually be executed.
   d. Are any problems created by updating the database through this view? If so, what are they? If not, why not?

2. A view, *SOFTPACK*, is to be defined. It consists of the package ID, package name, tag number, install date, software cost, and package cost for all packages currently installed on any PC.
   a. Write the view definition for *SOFTPACK*.
   b. Write an SQL query to retrieve the package ID, package name, tag number, and install date for all orders in *SOFTPACK* for customers whose software cost is more than the package cost.
   c. Convert the query from part b to the query that will actually be executed.
   d. Are any problems created by updating the database through this view? If so, what are they? If not, why not?

3. A view, *PCSFTCST*, is to be defined. It consists of the tag number of each PC along with the total cost of all software installed on the PC.
   a. Write the view definition for *PCSFTCST*.
   b. Write an SQL query to retrieve the tag number and total software cost for all PCs on which the total cost is over $100.
   c. Convert the query from part b to the query that will actually be executed.
   d. Are any problems created by updating the database through this view? If so, what are they? If not, why not?

4. Give SQL commands to grant the following privileges:
   a. User Stillwell must be able to retrieve data from the *PACKAGE* table.
   b. Users Webb and Bradley must be able to add new PCs and software records.
   c. User McKee must be able to change the cost of any package.
   d. User Thompson must be able to delete employees.
   e. All users must be able to retrieve package IDs and names.
   f. User Pool must be able to create an index on the *PC* table.
   g. User Locke must be able to change the structure of the *PACKAGE* table.
   h. User Scott must have all privileges on the *PC*, *SOFTWARE*, and *PACKAGE* tables.

    i. User Richards must be permitted to access any data concerning database packages but not to access data concerning any other parts.

5. User Stillwell is no longer to be able to retrieve data from the *PACKAGE* table. Give the SQL command necessary to revoke this privilege.

6. Give the SQL commands necessary to create the following indexes:
   a. Create a unique index on the *PACKID* column within the *PACKAGE* table. Call the index *PACKAGEIND*.
   b. Create an index called *PACKAGEIND2* on the *PACKTYPE* column within the *PACKAGE* table.
   c. Create an index called *PACKAGEIND3* on the *PACKTYPE, PACKVER* combination in the *PACKAGE* table.
   d. Create an index for the *PACKAGE* table called *PACKAGEIND4* on the combination of package type and descending cost.

7. The index called *PACKAGEIND3* is no longer necessary. Give the SQL command to delete it.

8. Find the following information from the system catalog:
   a. List the name, creator, and column count of all tables known to the system.
   b. List all the columns in the *PACKAGE* table as well as their associated data types.
   c. List all tables that contain a column called *EMPNUM*.
   d. List the name of all indexes in the system. Along with each index, list the name of the corresponding table as well as the creator of the index.
   e. List the name of all indexes associated with the *EMPLOYEE* table.
   f. Find the data type of the column called *EMPPHONE*.

9. Write a CREATE TABLE command for the *PACKAGE* table that will ensure that the only values entered for *PACKTYPE* are Accounting, Database, Spreadsheet, or Word Processing. The CREATE TABLE command should also indicate that *PACKID* is the primary key.

10. Write a CREATE TABLE command for the *SOFTWARE* table. The CREATE TABLE command should also indicate that the combination of *TAGNUM* and *PACKID* is the primary key, TAGNUM is a foreign key that must match the primary key of the PC table, and PACKID is a foreign key that must match the primary key of a the COMPUTER table.

EXERCISES (Movies)

1. Define a view called *SMALLMMB*. It consists of the customer number, name, address, city, state, number of rentals, and number of bonus units for all members who have rented less than 20 tapes.
   a. Write the view definition for *SMALLMMB*.
   b. Write an SQL query to retrieve the number and name of all members in *SMALLMMB* who have earned bonus units (that is, *BONUS* is greater than 0).

     c. Convert the query from part b to the query that will actually be executed.

     d. Are any problems created by updating the database through this view? If so, what are they? If not, why not?

2. Define a view called *MOVDIR*. It consists of the movie number, movie title, movie type, director number, and director name for all movies currently on file.

     a. Write the view definition for *MOVDIR*.

     b. Write an SQL query to retrieve the movie number, movie title, director number, and director name for all movies in *MOVDIR* of type COMEDY.

     c. Convert the query from part b to the query that will actually be executed.

     d. Are any problems created by updating the database through this view? If so, what are they? If not, why not?

3. Define a view called *RNTNUM*. It consists of the number of rentals for a tape together with the number of tapes that have been rented that number of times. (For example, there are four tapes that have been rented twice, so this view would contain a row in which the number of rentals is two and the number of tapes is four.)

     a. Write the view definition for *RNTNUM*.

     b. Write an SQL query to retrieve the number of rentals and corresponding number of tapes for all rows in *RNTNUM* on which the number of tapes is greater than three.

     c. Convert the query from part b to the query that will actually be executed.

     d. Are any problems created by updating the database through this view? If so, what are they? If not, why not?

4. Give SQL commands to grant the following privileges:

     a. User Sanders must be able to retrieve data from the *MEMBER* table.

     b. Users Brea and Alanson must be able to add new members and tapes.

     c. User Miles must be able to change the number of rentals and bonus units for all members.

     d. User Perry must be able to delete members.

     e. All users must be able to retrieve movies' numbers, titles, and movie types.

     f. User McLean must be able to create an index on the *TAPE* table.

     g. User Stapleton must be able to change the structure of the *MEMBER* table.

     h. User Hanks must have all privileges on the *MOVIE*, *MEMBER*, and *TAPE* tables.

     i. User Standish must be able to access any data concerning members who live in Carson, but not to access data concerning any other members.

5. User Sanders is no longer to be able to retrieve data from the *MEMBER* table. Give the SQL command necessary to revoke this privilege.

6. Give SQL commands necessary to create the following indexes:

     a. Create a unique index on the *MVNUMB* column within the *MOVIE* table. The index is to be called *MOVIND*.

     b. Create an index called *MOVIND2* on the *MVTITLE* column within the *MOVIE* table.

    c. Create a unique index called *MOVSTIND* on the *MVNUMB, STARNUMB* combination in the *MOVSTAR* table.

    d. Create an index for the *MOVIE* table called *MOVIND3* on the combination of movie type and descending number of nominations.

7. The index called *MOVIND3* is no longer necessary. Give the SQL command to delete it.

8. Find the following information from the system catalog:

    a. List the name, creator, and column count of all tables known to the system.

    b. List all the columns in the *MEMBER* table as well as their associated data types.

    c. List all tables that contain a column called *MMBNUMB*.

    d. List the name of all indexes in the system. Along with each index, list the name of the corresponding table as well as the creator of the index.

    e. List the name of all indexes associated with the *MOVIE* table.

    f. Find the data type of the column called *MVTITLE*.

9. Write a CREATE TABLE command for the *MOVIE* table that will ensure that the only values entered for *MVTYPE* are COMEDY, SUSPEN, RELIGI, SCI FI, HORROR, or DRAMA. The CREATE TABLE command should also indicate that *MVNUMB* is the primary key and that *DIRNUMB* is a foreign key that must match the primary key of the *DIRECTOR* table.

Embedded SQL

OBJECTIVES

When you have completed this chapter, you should understand the following:

1. How SQL can be embedded in a program in a language such as COBOL.
2. How to retrieve single rows using embedded SQL.
3. How to update a table using embedded INSERT, UPDATE, and DELETE commands.
4. How to use cursors to retrieve multiple rows in embedded SQL.
5. How to update a database using cursors.
6. How to handle errors in programs containing embedded SQL commands.

INTRODUCTION

So far, we have discussed the use of SQL only in a stand-alone mode (that is, an SQL query is entered and executed, results are produced, and the process terminates). It is possible to embed SQL commands in other languages, such as COBOL, thus bringing to these other languages all the benefits of SQL.

In the following discussion, we examine the method of embedding SQL within COBOL. The process of embedding SQL in other languages is similar. If you are not familiar with COBOL, don't worry. We're not interested in the details of COBOL, but rather, in the manner in which SQL commands can be embedded in it. If you simply treat the COBOL commands as a form of pseudocode, you should be able to understand the material in this chapter and apply it to languages familiar to you. Since we are focusing on the use of SQL, we will not get fancy with other aspects of the language. In particular, we will use simple ACCEPT and DISPLAY statements for input and output.

A COBOL program in which SQL commands are embedded will have additional statements in both the DATA and PROCEDURE divisions beyond the standard COBOL statements. In both cases, these new statements are preceded by

```
EXEC SQL
```

and followed by

```
END-EXEC
```

giving the compiler an easy way to distinguish such statements from standard COBOL statements. In the DATA DIVISION (in particular, in the WORKING-STORAGE SECTION), the new statements declare the tables that will be used in processing the database, as well as a communications area for SQL, including items that allow SQL to communicate various aspects of processing with the program. Of particular interest is the item SQLCODE. After the execution of any SQL statement, SQLCODE contains a code indicating the fate of the statement that was executed. If the execution was normal, SQLCODE will be zero. If not, the value in SQLCODE will indicate the problem that occurred (for example, not finding any rows that satisfy the condition in a WHERE clause). Programs should check the value of SQLCODE after each SQL statement.

In the PROCEDURE DIVISION, the new statements will be essentially SQL statements, with some slight variations. The examples that follow illustrate the use of SQL to retrieve a single row, insert new rows, update existing rows, and delete existing rows. Finally, we examine how to retrieve multiple rows. (Executing a SELECT statement that retrieves more than one row presents a problem for a language such as COBOL, which is oriented toward processing one record at a time. Thus, we must take some special action in such situations.)

DATA DIVISION

Any tables to be processed must be declared in WORKING-STORAGE. This is accomplished by the DECLARE TABLE command, which is similar to the SQL CREATE TABLE command. To process the *PACKAGE* table, for example, we would code:

```
EXEC SQL
     DECLARE PACKAGE TABLE
            (PACKID        CHAR (4),
             PACKNAME      CHAR (20),
             PACKVER       DECIMAL (3,2),
             PACKTYPE      CHAR (15),
             PACKCOST      DECIMAL (5,2))
END-EXEC.
```

Optionally, if the description of the *PACKAGE* table were stored in a library under the name DECPACKAGE, we could use:

```
EXEC SQL
      INCLUDE DECPACKAGE
END-EXEC.
```

As we will see, in processing this table we will need regular COBOL variables corresponding to the columns in the table. For the *PACKAGE* table we might have, for example:

```
01 W-PACKAGE.
      03 W-PACKID              PIC X(4).
      03 W-PACKNAME            PIC X(20).
      03 W-PACKVER             PIC S9V9(2)      COMP-3.
      03 W-PACKTYPE            PIC X(15).
      03 W-PACKCOST            PIC S9(3)V9(2) COMP-3.
```

Since this description is standard COBOL, it is not preceded by EXEC SQL. We have deliberately changed the names by prefacing each one with W-(for work variable). This procedure is not required; it is legitimate to use the same names that are in the table declaration. But doing so enhances readability.

Finally, the SQL communication area (SQLCA) is used by the system to provide feedback to the program. In particular, it is this area that contains SQLCODE. The SQLCA is included by coding:

```
EXEC SQL
      INCLUDE SQLCA
END-EXEC.
```

There is only one other new type of entry that appears in the DATA DIVISION. It is called a cursor and is used for the multiple-row SELECT mentioned earlier. We will defer discussion of cursors until we investigate the problems associated with multiple-row retrieval.

PROCEDURE DIVISION

Before we look at examples of the use of SQL statements in the PROCEDURE DIVISION, some general comments are in order. First, normal COBOL variables may be used in SQL statements. Such variables are called **host variables**, that is, they are variables in the host language (in this case, COBOL). These variables must be preceded by colons. If *W-PACKNAME* is used *within an SQL statement*, for example, it will appear as *:W-PACKNAME*. For any other use, it will appear as the normal *W-PACKNAME*. Second, the results of SQL queries must be placed in host variables through the use of the INTO clause, as in:

```
SELECT PACKNAME
    INTO :W-PACKNAME
    FROM PACKAGE
    WHERE PACKID = 'SS11'
```

With this introduction, we will now turn to the examples.

Retrieve a Single Row and Column

Example 82: Obtain the name of package SS11 and place it in *W-PACKNAME*.

Since this retrieval is based on the primary key (*PACKID*), it does not pose any problem for a record-at-a-time language like COBOL. If SQL were used in a stand-alone mode, the query would be:

```
SELECT PACKNAME
    FROM PACKAGE
    WHERE PACKID = 'SS11'
```

In COBOL, the statement is only slightly different:

```
EXEC SQL
    SELECT PACKNAME
        INTO :W-PACKNAME
        FROM PACKAGE
        WHERE PACKID = 'SS11'
END-EXEC.
```

The only difference other than the required EXEC SQL and END-EXEC is the INTO clause, which indicates that the result is to be placed in the host variable, *W-PACKNAME*. This variable may now be used in any way it could be used in any other COBOL program. Its value could be printed in a report, displayed on a screen, compared with some other name, and so on.

Retrieve a Single Row and All Columns

Example 83: Obtain all information about the package whose ID is stored in the host variable *W-PACKID*.

After filling in *W-PACKID* with an appropriate COBOL statement, such as MOVE or ACCEPT, this requirement could be satisfied by using a formulation similar to the one in Example 82:

```
EXEC SQL
    SELECT PACKNAME, PACKVER, PACKTYPE, PACKCOST
        INTO :W-PACKNAME, :W-PACKVER, :W-PACKTYPE,
            :W-PACKCOST
        FROM PACKAGE
        WHERE PACKID = :W-PACKID
END-EXEC.
```

In this formulation, several columns are listed after the SELECT, and the corresponding host variables that will receive the values are listed after INTO. In addition, the host variable *W-PACKID* is used in the WHERE clause. Note that there was no need to select *PACKID* and place it in *W-PACKID*, since *W- PACKID* already contained the desired number.

Figure 7.1 shows a complete COBOL program to accomplish the task. Let's look at the numbered portions of the program.

Figure 7.1

Program to display employee information

```
      IDENTIFICATION DIVISION.
      PROGRAM-ID.     DSPEMP.

      ENVIRONMENT DIVISION.

      DATA DIVISION.

      WORKING-STORAGE SECTION.

1     01   STATUS-FLAGS.
           03   ARE-WE-DONE              PIC X(3).
                88  WE-ARE-DONE                         VALUE 'YES'.

2     01   W-EMPLOYEE.
           03   W-EMPNUM               PIC S9(3)        COMP-3.
           03   W-EMPNAME              PIC X(20).
           03   W-EMPPHONE             PIC 9(4).

3          EXEC SQL
               DECLARE EMPLOYEE TABLE
                 (EMPNUM          DECIMAL (3),
                  EMPNAME         CHAR (20),
                  EMPPHONE        DECIMAL (4))
           END-EXEC.

4          EXEC SQL
               INCLUDE SQLCA
           END-EXEC.

      PROCEDURE DIVISION.

      MAIN-PROGRAM.
           MOVE 'NO' TO ARE-WE-DONE.
           PERFORM MAIN-LOOP
               UNTIL WE-ARE-DONE.
           STOP RUN.

      MAIN-LOOP.
5          DISPLAY 'EMPLOYEE NUMBER (0 TO END): '.
           ACCEPT W-EMPNUM.
           IF W-EMPNUM = 0
               MOVE 'YES' TO ARE-WE-DONE
             ELSE
               PERFORM FIND-AND-DISPLAY-EMPLOYEE.
```

(continued)

Figure 7.1

Program to display
employee
information
(continued)

```
                        FIND-AND-DISPLAY-EMPLOYEE.
6                           EXEC SQL
                                SELECT EMPNUM, EMPNAME, EMPPHONE
                                    INTO :W-EMPNUM, :W-EMPNAME, :W-EMPPHONE
                                    FROM EMPLOYEE
                                    WHERE EMPNUM = :W-EMPNUM
                            END-EXEC.
7                           IF SQLCODE = 0
                                DISPLAY '                NAME: ', W-EMPNAME
                                DISPLAY '               PHONE: ', W-EMPPHONE
                            ELSE
                                DISPLAY 'THERE IS NO SUCH EMPLOYEE'.
```

Q & A

Question: Examine the program and then describe the effect of the numbered lines.

Answer:
1. This program contains a loop. The user can repeatedly display employees. The data item called *ARE-WE-DONE* is a flag that indicates that the user does not wish to display any more employees. (The user indicates that he or she is finished by entering an employee number of zero.)
2. The record called *W-EMPLOYEE* contains the host variables that store the employee data. Within *W-EMPLOYEE*, there is a field for each column in the employee table. The approach used here for naming these fields is to precede the name of the column in the table with *W-*.
3. This is the declaration of the *EMPLOYEE* table. Note that it is very similar to the CREATE TABLE command.
4. This statement is used to include the SQL communication area (SQLCA), the area that SQL uses to provide feedback to the program.
5. This is the main loop. In it, the user is asked to enter the number of the desired employee or zero in case no more employees are desired. If the user has entered zero, the flag *ARE-WE-DONE* is set to YES, indicating that the process is to terminate. If not, we will perform the paragraph called FIND-AND-DISPLAY-EMPLOYEE.
6. This embedded SELECT statement will select the desired employee and place the information about the employee in the indicated host variables.
7. If SQLCODE contains the number zero, the desired employee was successfully found, in which case we can display the information. If not, the employee is not in the database so we display an appropriate error message.

Figure 7.2 represents a slightly different version of the same program. The only difference here occurs on the line numbered 1. Instead of including the specific table declaration for *EMPLOYEE* in the program, as in the previous ver-

Figure 7.2

Program to display
employee
information
(version 2)

```
IDENTIFICATION DIVISION.
PROGRAM-ID.     DSPEMP.

ENVIRONMENT DIVISION.

DATA DIVISION.

WORKING-STORAGE SECTION.

01  STATUS-FLAGS.
    03  ARE-WE-DONE             PIC X(3).
        88  WE-ARE-DONE                            VALUE 'YES'.

01  W-EMPLOYEE.
    03  W-EMPNUM               PIC S9(3)       COMP-3.
    03  W-EMPNAME              PIC X(20).
    03  W-EMPPHONE             PIC 9(4).
```

1
```
     EXEC SQL
         INCLUDE DECEMPLOYEE
     END-EXEC.

     EXEC SQL
         INCLUDE SQLCA
     END-EXEC.
```

```
PROCEDURE DIVISION.

MAIN-PROGRAM.
    MOVE 'NO' TO ARE-WE-DONE.
    PERFORM MAIN-LOOP
        UNTIL WE-ARE-DONE.
    STOP RUN.

MAIN-LOOP.
    DISPLAY 'EMPLOYEE NUMBER (0 TO END): '.
    ACCEPT W-EMPNUM.
    IF W-EMPNUM = 0
        MOVE 'YES' TO ARE-WE-DONE
      ELSE
        PERFORM FIND-AND-DISPLAY-EMPLOYEE.

FIND-AND-DISPLAY-EMPLOYEE.
    EXEC SQL
        SELECT EMPNUM, EMPNAME, EMPPHONE
            INTO :W-EMPNUM, :W-EMPNAME, :W-EMPPHONE
            FROM EMPLOYEE
            WHERE EMPNUM = :W-EMPNUM
    END-EXEC.
    IF SQLCODE = 0
        DISPLAY '              NAME: ', W-EMPNAME
        DISPLAY '             PHONE: ', W-EMPPHONE
      ELSE
        DISPLAY 'THERE IS NO SUCH EMPLOYEE'.
```

sion, we simply use the statement INCLUDE DECEMPLOYEE. This assumes that the declaration has already been created and stored in the file *DECEMPLOYEE*.

Retrieve a Single Row from a Join

Example 84: Obtain the tag number, computer ID of the PC whose tag number is stored in the host variable W-TAGNUM as well as the number and name of the employee to whom the PC is assigned.

This query involves joining the *PC* and *EMPLOYEE* tables. Since the restriction involves the primary key of the *PC* table, and since each PC is related to exactly one employee, the result of the query will be a single row. The method for handling this query is thus similar to that for the preceding queries. The SELECT command would be formulated as:

```
EXEC SQL
    SELECT COMPID, EMPLOYEE.EMPNUM, EMPNAME
        INTO :W-COMPID, :W-EMPNUM, :W-EMPNAME
        FROM PC, EMPLOYEE
        WHERE PC.EMPNUM = EMPLOYEE.EMPNUM
        AND PC.TAGNUM = :W-TAGNUM
END-EXEC.
```

Insert a Row into a Table

Example 85: Add a row to the package table. The package ID, name, version, type, and cost have already been placed in the variables *W-PACKID*, *W-PACKNAME*, *W-PACKVER*, *W-PACKTYPE*, and *W-PACKCOST*, respectively.

To insert a row into a table, we use the INSERT command. The values are contained in host variables, whose names must be preceded by colons, as follows:

```
EXEC SQL
    INSERT
        INTO PACKAGE
        VALUES (:W-PACKID, :W-PACKNAME, :W-PACKVER,
            :W-PACKTYPE, :W-PACKCOST)
END-EXEC.
```

The values currently in the host variables included in the INSERT statement will be used to add a new row to the *PACKAGE* table.

Figure 7.3 shows a complete COBOL program to add packages. Let's look at the numbered portions of the program.

Q & A

Question: Examine the program and then describe the effect of the numbered lines.

Answer: 1. This command performs the paragraph called OBTAIN-REMAINING-DATA, which obtains the rest of the data concerning the package from the user.

Figure 7.3

Program to add
packages

```
IDENTIFICATION DIVISION.
PROGRAM-ID.     ADDPACK.

ENVIRONMENT DIVISION.

DATA DIVISION.

01   STATUS-FLAGS.
     03   ARE-WE-DONE            PIC X(3).
          88   WE-ARE-DONE                      VALUE 'YES'.
     03   IS-DATA-VALID          PIC X(3).
          88 DATA-IS-VALID                      VALUE 'YES'.

01   W-PACKAGE.
     03   W-PACKID              PIC X(4)
     03   W-PACKNAME            PIC X(20).
     03   W-PACKVER             PIC S9V9(2).     COMP-3.
     03   W-PACKTYPE            PIC X(15).
     03   W-PACKCOST            PIC S9(3)V9(2)   COMP-3.

     EXEC SQL
          INCLUDE DECPACKAGE
     END-EXEC.

     EXEC SQL
          INCLUDE SQLCA
     END-EXEC.

PROCEDURE DIVISION.

MAIN-PROGRAM.
     MOVE 'NO' TO ARE-WE-DONE.
     PERFORM MAIN-LOOP
          UNTIL WE-ARE-DONE.
     STOP RUN.

MAIN-LOOP.
     DISPLAY 'PACKAGE ID (blank TO END): '.
     ACCEPT W-PACKID.
     IF W-PACKID = SPACE
          MOVE 'YES' TO ARE-WE-DONE
        ELSE
          PERFORM OBTAIN-REMAINING-DATA
          PERFORM VALIDATE-DATA
          IF DATA-IS-VALID
               PERFORM ADD-PACKAGE.

OBTAIN-REMAINING-DATA.
     DISPLAY 'PACKAGE NAME: '.
     ACCEPT W-PACKNAME.
     DISPLAY 'VERSION: '.
     ACCEPT W-PACKVER.
     DISPLAY 'TYPE: '.
     ACCEPT W-PACKTYPE.
     DISPLAY 'COST: '.
     ACCEPT W-PACKCOST.
```

1   (PERFORM OBTAIN-REMAINING-DATA)
2   (PERFORM VALIDATE-DATA)
3   (IF DATA-IS-VALID)
4   (DISPLAY 'PACKAGE NAME: ')

(continued)

Figure 7.3

Program to add
packages
(continued)

```
                              VALIDATE-DATA.
                                 MOVE 'YES' TO IS-DATA-VALID.
5                                EXEC SQL
                                    SELECT PACKNAME
                                       INTO :W-PACKNAME
                                       FROM PACKAGE
                                       WHERE PACKID = :W-PACKID
                                 END-EXEC.
6                                IF SQLCODE = 0
                                    MOVE 'NO' TO IS-DATA-VALID
                                    DISPLAY 'ERROR - DUPLICATE PACKAGE'.


                              ADD-PACKAGE.
7                                EXEC SQL
                                    INSERT
                                       INTO PACKAGE
                                       VALUES (:W-PACKID, :W-PACKNAME, :W-PACKVER,
                                              :W-PACKTYPE, :W-PACKCOST)
                                 END-EXEC.
```

2. The paragraph called VALIDATE-DATA ensures that the data entered by the user is valid. (The data is considered valid if the database does not contain a record with the same value of *PACKID*.) If the data is valid, the flag called IS-DATA-VALID will be set to YES. If not, it will be set to NO.
3. If the data is valid, we perform the paragraph called ADD-PACKAGE, which will add the data to the database.
4. For each field to be entered, this paragraph contains a prompt for the field (such as 'PACKAGE NAME: ') followed immediately by an ACCEPT command to obtain the desired data from the user.
5. The SELECT command is used to determine whether or not there was already a package in the database with the same ID.
6. If SQLCODE is zero, we successfully found such a package. In this case, we should not add another. We indicate this by setting *IS-DATA-VALID* to NO and displaying an error message.
7. This INSERT command adds the new row to the database.

In general, the paragraph called VALIDATE-DATA would be used to provide any sort of validation required. In a program to add PCs, for example, this paragraph could contain logic necessary to ensure that locations are "Accounting," "Sales," "Info Systems," or "Home." It could also contain logic to ensure that the employee number entered for the PC corresponded to an employee already in the database.

**Change a
Single Row
in a Table**

Example 86: Change the name of the package whose ID is currently stored in *W-PACKID* to the value currently stored in *W-PACKNAME*.

Again, the only difference between this example and the update examples encountered earlier is the use of host variables. The formulation is:

```
EXEC SQL
    UPDATE PACKAGE
        SET PACKNAME = :W-PACKNAME
        WHERE PACKID = :W-PACKID
END-EXEC.
```

**Change
Multiple
Rows in a
Table**

Example 87: Add the amount stored in the host variable *INCREASE- IN-COST* to the package cost of all packages of type Database.

Updating multiple rows does not pose any problem for COBOL. The formulation is:

```
EXEC SQL
    UPDATE PACKAGE
        SET PACKCOST = PACKCOST + :INCREASE-IN-COST
        WHERE PACKTYPE = 'Database'
END-EXEC.
```

**Delete a
Single Row
from a Table**

Example 88: Delete the computer whose ID is currently stored in *W-COMPID* from the *COMPUTER* table.

The formulation is:

```
EXEC SQL
    DELETE
        FROM COMPUTER
        WHERE COMPID = :W-COMPID
END-EXEC.
```

**Delete
Multiple
Rows from a
Table**

Sometimes we would like to delete more than one row from a table. If we have deleted an order from the *PC* table, for example, we also would want to delete all associated order lines from the *SOFTWARE* table, as in Example 89.

Example 89: Delete from the *SOFTWARE* table all records for the PC whose tag number is currently stored in the host variable *W-TAGNUM*.

The formulation is:

```
EXEC SQL
    DELETE
        FROM SOFTWARE
        WHERE TAGNUM = :W-TAGNUM
END-EXEC.
```

**Multiple-Row
Select—
Cursors**

All the examples so far have posed no problem for COBOL. The SELECT statements retrieved only individual rows. There was an UPDATE example in which multiple rows were updated and a DELETE example in which multiple rows were deleted, but these presented no difficulty. The SQL statements were executed and the updates or deletions took place. The program can move on to the next task.

What if a SELECT statement produced not one, but multiple, rows? What if, for example, the SELECT statement were to produce the computer ID and manufacturer's name of all computers whose processor type is stored in *W-PROCTYPE*? Could we formulate this query as shown?

```
EXEC SQL
      SELECT COMPID, MFGNAME
            INTO :W-COMPID, :W-MFGNAME
            FROM COMPUTER
            WHERE PROCTYPE = :W-PROCTYPE
END-EXEC.
```

A problem now emerges, stemming from the fact that COBOL is a language capable of processing only one record at a time, whereas this SQL command will produce a set of rows (records). Which computer ID and manufacturer name will be placed in *W-COMPID* and *W-MFGNAME* if 100 computers have been retrieved? Should we make both *W-COMPID* and *W-MFGNAME* arrays capable of holding multiple entries? If so, what should the size of these arrays be?

Fortunately, there is a solution to this problem, which involves the use of what is termed a **cursor**. (This is *not* the same as the cursor you see on your terminal screen.) Through the use of a cursor, COBOL can process the set of retrieved rows as though they were records in a sequential file. A cursor is essentially a pointer to a row in the collection of rows retrieved by an SQL statement. This pointer can be advanced one row at a time to provide sequential, record-at-a-time-type access to the retrieved rows.

Example 90: Retrieve the computer ID and manufacturer's name of all computers whose processor type is stored in the host variable *W-PROCTYPE*.

The first step in using a cursor is to declare the cursor and describe the associated query. We accomplish this in the WORKING-STORAGE SECTION of the DATA DIVISION, as follows:

```
EXEC SQL
      DECLARE COMPGROUP CURSOR FOR
            SELECT COMPID, MFGNAME
                FROM COMPUTER
                WHERE PROCTYPE = :W-PROCTYPE
END-EXEC.
```

This formulation does *not* cause the query to be executed at this time. It merely indicates that we have a cursor called *COMPGROUP* and that this cursor is associated with the indicated query.

Using a cursor in the PROCEDURE DIVISION involves three facets: OPEN,

FETCH, and CLOSE. Opening the cursor effectively causes the query to be executed and makes the results available to the program. Executing a fetch advances the pointer to the next row in the set of rows retrieved by the query and places the contents of this row in the indicated host variables. Finally, closing a cursor deactivates it. Data retrieved by the execution of the query is no longer available. The cursor could later be opened again and processing could begin anew. If any host variables used in making the selection were changed, however, the set of rows retrieved might be totally different.

The OPEN, FETCH, and CLOSE commands used in processing a cursor are analogous to the OPEN, READ, and CLOSE commands used in processing a sequential file. We will now examine how each of these commands is coded in COBOL.

OPEN.   The formulation for the OPEN command is

```
EXEC SQL
      OPEN COMPGROUP
END-EXEC.
```

Figure 7.4 shows the result of opening this cursor. In the figure, we are assuming that *W-PROCTYPE* has been set to 486DX before the OPEN statement was executed. Notice that prior to the OPEN, no rows were available. After the OPEN, two rows are now available to the program and we are positioned at the first row; that is, the next FETCH command will cause the contents of the first row to be placed in the indicated host variables.

Figure 7.4a

Before OPEN

COMPGROUP

COMPID	MFGNAME		W-COMPID	W-MFGNAME	SQLCODE
		← no rows to be fetched			0

Figure 7.4b

After OPEN, but before first FETCH

COMPGROUP

COMPID	MFGNAME		W-COMPID	W-MFGNAME	SQLCODE
B121	Bantam	← next row to be fetched			0
C007	Cody				

FETCH.   To fetch (get) the next row from a cursor, the FETCH command is used as follows:

```
EXEC SQL
      FETCH COMPGROUP
            INTO :W-COMPID, :W-MFGNAME
      END-EXEC.
```

Note that the INTO clause is associated with the FETCH command itself, not the query used in the definition of the cursor. The execution of that query will probably produce multiple rows. The execution of the FETCH command produces only a single row, so it is appropriate that the FETCH command causes data to be placed in the indicated host variables.

Figure 7.5 shows the result of three FETCH commands. Note that the first two are successful. In each case, the data from the appropriate row in the cursor is placed in the indicated host variables and SQLCODE is set to zero. The third FETCH is different, however, since there is no data to be fetched. In this case, the content of the host variables is left untouched and SQLCODE is set to 100.

Figure 7.5a

After first FETCH

COMPGROUP

COMPID	MFGNAME
B121	Bantam
C007	Cody

← next row to be fetched

W-COMPID	W-MFGNAME	SQLCODE
B121	Bantam	0

Figure 7.5b

After second FETCH

COMPGROUP

COMPID	MFGNAME
B121	Bantam
C007	Cody

← no more rows to be fetched

W-COMPID	W-MFGNAME	SQLCODE
C007	Cody	0

Figure 7.5c

Ater attempting a third FETCH (note SQLCODE is 100)

COMPGROUP

COMPID	MFGNAME
B121	Bantam
C007	Cody

← no more rows to be fetched

W-COMPID	W-MFGNAME	SQLCODE
C007	Cody	100

CLOSE. The formulation for the CLOSE command is

```
EXEC SQL
    CLOSE COMPGROUP
END-EXEC.
```

Figure 7.6 shows the result of closing the cursor: The data is no longer available.

Figure 7.6

After CLOSE

COMPGROUP

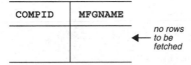

COMPID	MFGNAME

← no rows
to be
fetched

Figure 7.7 shows a complete COBOL program using this cursor. Let's examine the numbered portions of the program.

Figure 7.7

Program to display
computers with a
given processor

```
        IDENTIFICATION DIVISION.
        PROGRAM-ID.      COMPPROC.

        ENVIRONMENT DIVISION.

        DATA DIVISION.

        WORKING-STORAGE SECTION.

        01   STATUS-FLAGS.
             03   ARE-WE-DONE          PIC X(3).
                  88   WE-ARE-DONE                    VALUE 'YES'.

1       01 W-COMPUTER.
             03   W-COMPID             PIC X(4).
             03   W-MFGNAME            PIC X(6).
             03   W-MFGMODEL           PIC X(3).
             03   W-PROCTYPE           PIC X(6).

2           EXEC SQL
                INCLUDE DECCOMPUTER
            END-EXEC.

            EXEC SQL
                INCLUDE SQLCA
            END-EXEC.
```

(continued)

Figure 7.7

Program to display
computers with a
given processor
(continued)

3

```
EXEC SQL
     DECLARE COMPGROUP CURSOR FOR
         SELECT COMPID, MFGNAME
             FROM COMPUTER
                 WHERE PROCTYPE = :W-PROCTYPE
END EXEC.

PROCEDURE DIVISION.

MAIN-PROGRAM.
    MOVE 'NO' TO ARE-WE-DONE.
    PERFORM MAIN-LOOP
        UNTIL WE-ARE-DONE.
    STOP RUN.

MAIN-LOOP.
    DISPLAY 'PROCESSOR TYPE (BLANK TO END):'.
    ACCEPT W-PROCTYPE.
    IF W-PROCTYPE = SPACE
        MOVE 'YES' TO ARE-WE-DONE
      ELSE
        PERFORM FIND-COMPUTERS.

FIND-COMPUTERS.
```
4
```
    EXEC SQL
        OPEN COMPGROUP
    END-EXEC.
```
5
```
    PERFORM FIND-A-COMPUTER                     UNTIL SQLCODE = 100.
```
6
```
    EXEC SQL
        CLOSE COMPGROUP
    END-EXEC.

FIND-A-COMPUTER.
```
7
```
    EXEC SQL
        FETCH COMPGROUP
            INTO :W-COMPID, :W-MFGNAME
    END-EXEC.
```
8
```
    IF SQLCODE = 0
        DISPLAY '      COMPUTER ID: ', W-COMPID
        DISPLAY 'MANUFACTURER NAME: ', W-MFGNAME.
```

Q & A

Question: Examine the program and then describe the effect of the numbered lines.

Answer:
1. The appropriate host variables for computer data are declared as a record called *W-COMPUTER*.
2. The description of the computer table is stored in *DECCOMPUTER,* so this name appears in an INCLUDE statement.
3. This statement gives the declaration of the cursor (*COMPGROUP*).

4. This statement opens the cursor, making the desired data available to the program.
5. This statement performs the paragraph called FIND-A-COMPUTER until SQLCODE is set to 100. Recall that this will happen when all rows have been fetched and an attempt is made to fetch another row.
6. This statement closes the cursor.
7. This is the FETCH command that will place the information from the next row in the cursor into the indicated host variables. If no more rows exist, SQLCODE will be set to 100.
8. If SQLCODE is zero, this indicates that a row was found and the data can be displayed.

More Complex Cursors

The formulation of the query to define the cursor in the previous example was relatively simple. Any SQL query is legitimate in a cursor definition. In fact, the more complicated the requirements for retrieval, the more numerous the benefits derived by the programmer who uses embedded SQL. Consider the query in Example 91.

Example 91: For each installation of the package whose ID is stored in *W-PACKID*, list the package ID, the package name, the installation date, the tag number of the PC on which it was installed, the computer ID of the PC, the number of the employee to whom the PC is assigned, and the name of the employee. Sort the results by employee number.

Opening and closing the cursor will be accomplished exactly as in the previous example. The only difference in the FETCH command will be a different set of host variables in the INTO clause. Thus, the only real distinction is in the definition of the cursor itself. In this case, the cursor definition would be:

```
EXEC SQL
    DECLARE ORDGROUP CURSOR FOR
        SELECT SOFTWARE.PACKID, PACKNAME, INSTDATE,
               SOFTWARE.TAGNUM, COMPUTER.COMPID, PC.EMPNUM, EMPNAME
               FROM SOFTWARE, PACKAGE, PC, EMPLOYEE
               WHERE PACKAGE.PACKID = :W-PACKID
               AND   PACKAGE.PACKID = SOFTWARE.PACKID
               AND   PC.TAGNUM = SOFTWARE.TAGNUM
               AND   EMPLOYEE.EMPNUM = PC.EMPNUM
               ORDER BY EMPLOYEE.EMPNUM
    END-EXEC.
```

Advantages of Cursors

The retrieval requirements in Example 91 are quite involved. Yet, beyond coding the preceding cursor declaration, the programmer needn't worry about the mechanics of obtaining the necessary data or placing it in the right order. This will occur automatically when the cursor is opened. It is as though a sequential file already exists with precisely the right data in it, sorted in the right order. This leads to three main advantages.

First, the coding in the program is greatly simplified. Second, the system optimizer will determine the best way to execute the query. The programmer doesn't have to be concerned with the best way to pull the data together. In addition, if an underlying structure changes, for example, if an additional index is created, the system optimizer will determine the best way to execute the query in view of the new structure. The program does not have to change at all. Third, if the database structure changes so that the necessary information is still obtainable but through a query formatted differently, the only change required in the program is the cursor definition in WORKING-STORAGE. The PROCEDURE DIVISION code will not be affected.

Updating Cursors

Rows encountered in processing cursors may be updated. In order to indicate that an update is required, an additional clause, the FOR UPDATE OF clause, is included in the cursor definition. For example, consider the update requirement in Example 92.

Example 92: Subtract 5% from the package cost of each package whose package name is stored in W-PACKNAME and for which there are three or more installations at Chazy. Subtract 2% from the package cost for all such packages with two installations. Write the ID and name of all such packages for which there is only one installation.

In this example, the cursor declaration would be:

```
EXEC SQL
    DECLARE PACKGROUP CURSOR FOR
        SELECT PACKID, PACKNAME, PACKCOST, NUMINST
            FROM PACKAGE
            WHERE PACKNAME = :W-PACKNAME
            FOR UPDATE OF PACKCOST
END-EXEC.
```

In order to update the credit limit, we include the clause FOR UPDATE OF PACKCOST in the declaration. The PROCEDURE DIVISION code for the OPEN and CLOSE will be the same one discussed before. The code to fetch a row, determine whether it was actually fetched, and then take appropriate action would be:

```
EXEC SQL
    FETCH PACKGROUP
        INTO :W-PACKID, :W-PACKNAME, :W-PACKCOST,
            :W-NUMINST
```

```
                    END-EXEC.
                    IF SQLCODE = 100
                          MOVE ''NO'' TO ARE-THERE-MORE-PACKAGES
                       ELSE
                          PERFORM PACKAGE-UPDATE.

                PACKAGE-UPDATE.
                    IF W-NUMINST <= 1
                          DISPLAY W-PACKID, W-PACKNAME
                       ELSE IF W-NUMINST = 2
                          EXEC SQL
                              UPDATE PACKAGE
                                    SET PACKCOST = .98 * PACKCOST
                                    WHERE CURRENT OF PACKGROUP
                          END-EXEC
                       ELSE
                          EXEC SQL
                              UPDATE PACKAGE
                                    SET PACKCOST = .95 * PACKCOST
                                    WHERE CURRENT OF PACKGROUP
                          END-EXEC.
```

The preceding code will be in a loop that is performed until the flag ARE-THERE-MORE-PACKAGES is set to NO. The FETCH command will either make the next retrieved row available to the program with the values placed in the variables *W-PACKID*, *W-PACKNAME*, *W-PACKCOST*, and *W-NUMINST*, or it will set SQLCODE to 100 to indicate that no more rows were retrieved. The code that comes after the FETCH command will set the flag to NO if SQLCODE is 100. If not, the UPDATE routine will be performed.

In the UPDATE routine, the number of installations is first compared with 1. If the number of installations is less than or equal to 1, a message is printed. If not, it is compared with 2. If the number of installations is equal, the package cost is updated by multiplying it by .98 (98%), which decreases the cost by 2%. If neither of these conditions is true, the number of installations must be 3 or more. In that case, the package cost is updated by multiplying it by .95 (95%), which decreases the cost by 5%.

Notice the clause WHERE CURRENT OF PACKGROUP, which indicates that the update is to apply only to the row just fetched. Without this clause and in the absence of any WHERE clause to restrict the scope of the update, *all* package costs would be updated at once.

ERROR HANDLING

Checking SQLCODE

Programs must be prepared to handle exceptional conditions that may arise when the database is being accessed. Since any problem encountered is communicated through a value in SQLCODE, one way to handle such conditions is to check the value in SQLCODE after each executable SQL statement and take appropriate action based on the problem indicated. With all the conceivable conditions, this method becomes cumbersome. Fortunately, there is another way to handle such conditions.

Using WHENEVER

Two distinct types of conditions may arise. One type consists of unusual but normal conditions, such as not retrieving any data to match a given condition, attempting to store a row that violates a duplicates clause, and so on. The value in SQLCODE for such conditions is a positive number. The appropriate action may be to print an error message and go on. In fact, for one, END OF DATA (SQLCODE 100), the appropriate action is probably termination of some loop and continuation of the rest of the program. Not even an error message is required.

The other type of condition is far more serious. These are the abnormal and unexpected conditions or the fatal ones. Examples of this type include no more room in the database, a damaged database, and so on. The value in SQLCODE for such conditions is a negative number. The appropriate action is usually to print a final message that indicates which problem occurred and to terminate the program.

The WHENEVER statement can be used to handle these errors in a global way. The following example of the WHENEVER statement illustrates a typical way of handling these conditions in a program:

```
EXEC SQL
     WHENEVER SQLERROR      GOTO ERROR-PROCESSING-ROUTINE
END-EXEC.
EXEC SQL
     WHENEVER SQLWARNING    CONTINUE
END-EXEC.
EXEC SQL
     WHENEVER NOT FOUND     CONTINUE
END-EXEC.
```

In the WHENEVER statement, SQLERROR represents the abnormal or fatal conditions (SQLCODE < 0), SQLWARNING represents the unusual but normal conditions (SQLCODE > 0), and NOT FOUND represents the special warning END OF DATA (SQLCODE = 100). The WHENEVER statement ends either with GOTO followed by a section or paragraph name or with the word CONTINUE. This statement indicates how each of these conditions should be handled if and when it occurs.

The preceding WHENEVER statements indicate that if a fatal condition occurs, the program is to proceed immediately to a paragraph (or section) called ERROR-PROCESSING-ROUTINE. Such a paragraph has probably been constructed by the organization and will be the same in each program that uses embedded SQL. Typically, it would contain statements to display the SQLCODE together with any other information deemed useful in tracking down the problem, followed by a STOP RUN. With this paragraph in place, the remainder of the program does not have to check continually for all possible errors of this type.

If an unusual but normal condition or the special NOT FOUND condition arises, however, processing continues without any special action being taken. This means that appropriate tests of SQLCODE must be included at appropriate places. While these tests can also be accomplished through the WHENEVER clause, doing the testing ourselves provides a cleaner structure for the program. The built-in GOTO of the WHENEVER clause can undermine the attempt to create well-structured programs.

SUMMARY

Following is a summary of the material covered in Chapter 7:

1. To embed SQL commands in a COBOL program, precede the SQL command with EXEC SQL and follow it with END-EXEC.
2. Statements to define the tables to be accessed must appear in the DATA DIVISION.
3. The DATA DIVISION must contain the statement INCLUDE SQLCA, which allows access to the SQL communication area.
4. Host language variables (that is, variables that are not columns within a table) may be used in embedded SQL commands. If they are applied, they must be preceded with a colon.
5. SELECT statements may be used as embedded SQL commands in COBOL programs provided they cause only a single row to be retrieved.
6. To place the results of a SELECT statement into host language variables, employ the INTO clause in the SELECT command.
7. INSERT, UPDATE, and DELETE statements may be used in COBOL programs even if they affect more than one row.
8. If a SELECT statement will retrieve more than one row, it must be used to define a cursor, which will then be used to furnish COBOL with one row at a time.
9. To activate a cursor, use the OPEN command, which will execute the query in the cursor definition.
10. To furnish the next row to COBOL, use the FETCH command.
11. To deactivate the cursor, use the CLOSE command. The rows initially retrieved will no longer be available to COBOL.
12. Data in the tables on which a cursor is based may be updated by including the clause WHERE CURRENT OF cursor-name in the update statement. This will update only the current row (the row most recently fetched).
13. To check to see if an error has occurred, you can examine the value in SQLCODE.

14. Rather than checking SQLCODE at all the places in the program where errors occur, you can use the WHENEVER clause.

EXERCISES (Chazy Associates)

Note: Your instructor may substitute another language for COBOL in the following exercises.

1. Assuming that the appropriate entries have been made in the DATA DIVISION of a COBOL program, give the procedure division code for each of the following:
   a. Obtain the name and phone number of the employee whose number is currently stored in *W-EMPNUM*. Place these values in the variables *W-EMPNAME* and *W-EMPPHONE*, respectively.
   b. Obtain the computer ID, the employee number, the employee name, and the location of the PC for the PC whose tag number is currently stored in *W-TAGNUM*. Place these values in the variables *W-COMPID*, *W-EMPNUM*, *W-EMPNAME* and *W-LOCATION*, respectively.
   c. Add a row to the *PC* table. The data is currently stored in the fields within the *W-PC* record.
   d. Change the name of the employee whose number is stored in *W-EMPNUM* to the value currently found in *W-EMPNAME*.
   e. Increase the cost of all database packages by 5%.
   f. Delete the employee whose number is stored in *W-EMPNUM*.
2. Let's assume we wish to retrieve all details about all packages whose type is stored in *W-PACKTYPE*.
   a. Write an appropriate cursor description.
   b. Give all statements that will be included in the PROCEDURE DIVISION and that relate to processing the database through this cursor.
   c. Write the additional PROCEDURE DIVISION code that will update any of these packages whose type is Word Processing by adding 5% to the cost and any packages whose type is Database by adding 10% to the cost. (The cursor must be used in the answer.)
3. If you have access to embedded SQL, write and run the programs discussed in Exercises 1 and 2.

EXERCISES (Movies)

Note: Your instructor may substitute another language for COBOL in the following exercises.

1. Assuming that the appropriate entries have been made in the DATA DIVISION of a COBOL program, give the procedure division code for each of the following:

a. Obtain the name and birthplace of the star whose number is currently stored in *W-STARNUM*. Place these values in the variables *W-STARNAME* and *W-BRTHPLCE*, respectively.

b. Obtain the movie title, type, director number, and director name of the movie whose number is currently stored in *W-MVNUM*. Place these values in the variables *W-MVTITLE*, *W-MVTYPE*, *W-DIRNUM*, and *W-DIRNAME*, respectively.

c. Add a row to the *MEMBER* table. First, prompt the user to enter desired data for the new member and place the desired data in fields called *W-MMBNUM*, *W-MMBNAME*, *W-MMBADDR*, *W-MMBCTY*, *W-MMBST*, *W-NUMRENT*, *W-BONUS*, and *W-JOINDATE*. Then use this data to add a row to the table.

d. Change the name of the member whose number is stored in *W-MMBNUM* to the value currently found in *W-MMBNAME*.

e. Increase the bonus for the member whose number is stored in *W-MMBNUM* by the amount currently stored in *W-ADD-BONUS*.

f. Delete the tape whose number is stored in *W-TPNUM*.

2. We wish to retrieve all tapes that are currently rented by the member whose number is stored in *W-MMBNUM*. For each tape, we need the tape number, the purchase date, and the number of times the tape has been rented. In addition, we need the number and title of the movie on the tape as well as the number and name of the director of the movie.

a. Write an appropriate cursor description.

b. Give all statements that will be included in the PROCEDURE DIVISION and that relate to processing the database through this cursor.

c. Write the additional PROCEDURE DIVISION code that will ask the user for a member number. If the member number entered is zero, the program should terminate. Otherwise, the program should display all the desired data and then ask for a new member number. (The cursor must be used in the answer.)

3. If you have access to embedded SQL, write and run the programs discussed in Exercises 1 and 2.

8

SQL2

OBJECTIVES

When you have completed this chapter, you should understand the following:

1. How to support transactions in SQL2.
2. How to create and use domains in SQL2.
3. How to use the CASE clause in SELECT and UPDATE commands.
4. How to use the INTERSECT and EXCEPT commands.
5. How to use special SQL2 features to provide additional integrity support.
6. The role of SQLSTATE and its advantages compared with SQLCODE.

INTRODUCTION

This chapter is devoted to the most recent version of SQL, which is not yet fully supported by all SQL vendors. This version supports all the material from the previous chapters and incorporates several new features as well. It is often called SQL2, although it is also referred to as SQL/92 (or SQL-92). In this chapter, we look at some of the most important of the new features. We review support for transactions at the new CASE clause and at domain support. We cover the new approach to joins as well as new commands for intersection and difference. We also discuss additional integrity support features that expand on the Integrity Enhancement Feature (IEF) presented in Chapter 6. Finally, we explain SQLSTATE, a parameter designed to correct some of the problems with the SQLCODE parameter covered in Chapter 7.

TRANSACTIONS

A **logical transaction** (often simply called a *transaction*) is a sequence of steps that accomplishes a single task (or, at least, what feels to the user like a single task). The following are some examples of logical transactions: add an employee, enter an order, enroll a student in a course, deactivate an employee, or increase the units on hand of a particular part by 50. To a user, these all seem to be single tasks. Accomplishing such a so-called single task, however, may require many changes to be made to the database. Provided all the changes are indeed made, everything is fine. We would have *severe* problems if some were made and others were not.

To solve this problem, SQL2 includes two new commands, COMMIT and ROLLBACK. When all the updates for a transaction have been complete, you would execute the command

```
COMMIT
```

At this point, all the updates would be made permanent and available to other users.

If you find you cannot complete all the updates, you would execute the command

```
ROLLBACK
```

All updates since the last COMMIT would be undone. Incidentally, if SQL2 detects a problem, such as a program abort or a computer problem, it will perform an automatic rollback.

CASE

SQL2 includes a CASE expression that can be used in SQL commands. The form of the expression is

```
CASE
   WHEN condition₁ THEN result₁
   WHEN condition₂ THEN result₂
         ...
   WHEN conditionₙ THEN resultₙ
END
```

A CASE expression can be used in SELECT statements as well as UPDATE statements. Example 93 illustrates the use of a CASE expression in a SELECT statement, and Example 94 illustrates its use in an UPDATE statement.

Example 93: List the package ID and package name of all packages. You also want to list the word "HIGH" if the package cost is over $400; "MEDIUM" if the package cost is more than $200, but less than $400; "LOW" if the cost is more than $100, but less than $200; or "VERY LOW" if the cost is less than $100. To do so, you could use the following SELECT command:

```
SELECT PACKID, PACKNAME,
    CASE
      WHEN PACKCOST >= 400 THEN 'HIGH'
      WHEN PACKCOST >= 200 AND PACKCOST < 400 THEN 'MEDIUM'
      WHEN PACKCOST >= 100 AND PACKCOST < 200 THEN 'LOW'
      ELSE 'VERY LOW'
    END
    FROM PACKAGE
```

Example 94: Assume that there is an additional column in the *PACKAGE* table, *NUMINST*, that indicates the number of units of the package that are currently installed. Subtract 5% from the package cost of each package for which there are three (3) or more installations at Chazy. Subtract 2% from the package cost for packages with two (2) installations. Subtract 1% from the package cost for all other packages.

```
UPDATE PACKAGE
    SET PACKCOST = CASE
      WHEN NUMINST >= 3 THEN PACKCOST = .95 * PACKCOST
      WHEN NUMINST = 2 THEN PACKCOST = .98 * PACKCOST
      ELSE PACKCOST = .99 * PACKCOST
```

DOMAINS

A **domain** is a pool of the possible values for a given attribute. By indicating the data type of an attribute, you are effectively indicating a domain, although not a very specific one. A data type of CHAR(10), for example, indicates that the value for the corresponding attribute must be a character string of length 10. It does not indicate anything more specific than that.

On the other hand, domains can be much more specific. We could create a domain called *LOCATIONS*, for example, that contains one of four values: "Accounting," "Sales," "Info Systems," or "Home." Only values from the domain for a particular attribute will be accepted in any updates to the database.

Example 95: Create the LOCATIONS domain.

The CREATE DOMAIN command in SQL2 creates a domain. It is CREATE DOMAIN followed first by the name of the domain and then by the data type.

It then contains a CHECK clause that gives a condition that the values in the domain must satisfy. To create the *LOCATIONS* domain described in the previous paragraph, for example, the command would be:

```
CREATE DOMAIN LOCATIONS CHAR(12)
     CHECK (VALUE = 'Accounting' OR VALUE = 'Sales' OR
            VALUE = 'Info Systems' OR VALUE = 'Home')
```

The condition in the CHECK clause indicates that the value must be 'Accounting, 'Sales,' 'Info Systems,' or 'Home.' Once the domain is created, it can be used in CREATE TABLE command in place of data types. The following portion of a CREATE TABLE command uses the *LOCATIONS* domain to describe the attribute called *LOCATION*, for example:

```
CREATE TABLE PC
     .
     .
     LOCATION       LOCATIONS
     .
     .
```

JOINS

The Join operation covered in Chapter 4 represents a type of Join called the **natural join**. Suppose, for example, that we want to join the following tables:

PC

TAGNUM	COMPID	EMPNUM
32808	M759	611
37691	B121	124
57772	C007	567
59836	B221	124
77740	M759	567
80269	C007	852

and

EMPLOYEE

EMPNUM	EMPNAME
124	Alvarez, Ramon
258	Lopez, Maria
567	Feinstein, Betty
611	Dinh, Melissa

Notice that there is a PC, 80269, that does not match any employee. There is also an employee, 611, that does not match any PC.

To join these tables using the type of command given in Chapter 4, we would type:

```
SELECT TAGNUM, COMPID, EMPLOYEE.EMPNUM, EMPNAME
     FROM PC, EMPLOYEE
     WHERE PC.EMPNUM = EMPLOYEE.EMPNUM
```

The result would be:

TAGNUM	COMPID	EMPNUM	EMPNAME
32808	M759	611	Dinh, Melissa
37691	B121	124	Alvarez, Ramon
57772	C007	567	Feinstein, Betty
59836	B221	124	Alvarez, Ramon
77740	M759	567	Feinstein, Betty

If there is a row in one table that does not match any row in the other table, it will not appear in the result of the join. Thus, employee 258, Maria Lopez, and the PC with tag number 80269 do not appear, since they do not match anything.

Example 96: Use SQL2 commands to join the tables.

In SQL2, there is a clause to join tables. The clause is JOIN and it appears in the FROM clause of a SQL command. To do a natural join, precede the word JOIN with the word NATURAL, as in the following:

```
SELECT TAGNUM, COMPID, EMPNUM, EMPNAME
     FROM PC NATURAL JOIN EMPLOYEE
```

This command will automatically join the *PC* and *EMPLOYEE* tables on the matching columns (*EMPNUM*).

Another type of join, the **outer join**, differs from the natural join only for rows in the original tables that do not match any row in the other table. In the natural join, these rows are eliminated. In the outer join, they are maintained, and values of the columns from the other table are left vacant, or **null**. You can choose whether to include such values from the table on the left (a **left outer join**), the table on the right (a **right outer join**), or both (a **full outer join**). Examples of these three follow:

Example 97: Perform a left outer join in SQL2.

```
SELECT TAGNUM, COMPID, EMPNUM, EMPNAME
    FROM PC LEFT OUTER JOIN EMPLOYEE
```

RESULT:

TAGNUM	COMPID	EMPNUM	EMPNAME
32808	M759	611	Dinh, Melissa
37691	B121	124	Alvarez, Ramon
57772	C007	567	Feinstein, Betty
59836	B221	124	Alvarez, Ramon
77740	M759	567	Feinstein, Betty
80269	C007	852	-

Example 98: Perform a right outer join in SQL2.

```
SELECT TAGNUM, COMPID, EMPNUM, EMPNAME
    FROM PC RIGHT OUTER JOIN EMPLOYEE
```

TEMP

TAGNUM	COMPID	EMPNUM	EMPNAME
32808	M759	611	Dinh, Melissa
37691	B121	124	Alvarez, Ramon
57772	C007	567	Feinstein, Betty
59836	B221	124	Alvarez, Ramon
77740	M759	567	Feinstein, Betty
-	-	258	Lopez, Maria

Example 99: Perform a full outer join in SQL2.

```
SELECT TAGNUM, COMPID, EMPNUM, EMPNAME
    FROM PC FULL OUTER JOIN EMPLOYEE
```

TEMP

TAGNUM	COMPID	EMPNUM	EMPNAME
32808	M759	611	Dinh, Melissa
37691	B121	124	Alvarez, Ramon
57772	C007	567	Feinstein, Betty
59836	B221	124	Alvarez, Ramon
77740	M759	567	Feinstein, Betty
–	–	258	Lopez, Maria
80269	C007	852	–

UNION, INTERSECTION, DIFFERENCE

In Chapter 4, you learned how to use the union operator to list the computer ID and manufacturer's name of all computers that either have a 486DX processor or have been assigned for home use, or both. The command to do so is

```
SELECT COMPID, MFGNAME
    FROM COMPUTER
    WHERE PROCTYPE = '486DX'
UNION
SELECT COMPUTER.COMPID, MFGNAME
    FROM COMPUTER, PC
    WHERE COMPUTER.COMPID = PC.COMPID
    AND LOCATION = 'Home'
```

Since there was no intersection operator, you had to use a different approach to list the computer ID and manufacturer's name of all computers that have a 486DX processor *and* have been assigned for home use. The command given in Chapter 4 for this example was

```
SELECT COMPID, MFGNAME
    FROM COMPUTER
    WHERE PROCTYPE = '486DX'
    AND COMPID IN
        (SELECT·COMPID
            FROM PC
            WHERE LOCATION = 'Home')
```

In SQL2, however, there is an INTERSECT operator, which enables you to use a command similar to the version with UNION:

Example 100: Perform an intersection in SQL2.

```
SELECT COMPID, MFGNAME
      FROM COMPUTER
      WHERE PROCTYPE = '486DX'
INTERSECT
SELECT COMPUTER.COMPID, MFGNAME
      FROM COMPUTER, PC
      WHERE COMPUTER.COMPID = PC.COMPID
      AND LOCATION = 'Home'
```

Similarly, there was no operator for Difference, so to list the computer ID and manufacturer's name of all computers that have a 486DX processor *but have not* been assigned for home use, you used the following command:

```
SELECT COMPID, MFGNAME
      FROM COMPUTER
      WHERE PROCTYPE = '486DX'
      AND COMPID IN
          (SELECT COMPID
               FROM PC
               WHERE LOCATION = 'Home')
```

In SQL2, there is a corresponding operator. Instead of DIFFERENCE, as you might expect, the operator is EXCEPT, as the following example shows:

Example 101: Perform a difference in SQL2.

```
SELECT COMPID, MFGNAME
      FROM COMPUTER
      WHERE PROCTYPE = '486DX'
EXCEPT
SELECT COMPUTER.COMPID, MFGNAME
      FROM COMPUTER, PC
      WHERE COMPUTER.COMPID = PC.COMPID
      AND LOCATION = 'Home'
```

INTEGRITY SUPPORT

The Integrity Enhancement Feature (IEF) provides integrity support, that is, support to ensure that data in the database followed certain rules. SQL2 provides additional integrity support in two ways. The first is through **assertions,** or independent statements (that is, not a part of any CREATE TABLE statement), that specify rules for the data. The second is through additional rules that can be specified for foreign keys.

Assertions have the form:

```
CREATE ASSERTION assertion-name CHECK condition
```

Each assertion must be assigned a name, which follows CREATE ASSER-
TION in the command. The condition that the data must satisfy follows the word
CHECK.

Suppose, for example, you want to create an assertion called *A1* to indicate
that the cost of each package in the *PACKAGE* table (*PACKCOST*) must be at least
as big as the largest software cost (*SOFTCOST*) on software records for that
package. Another way of stating this is that there should not be any row in the
PACKAGE table on which the package cost is less than the largest software cost
for any matching record in the *SOFTWARE* table. The CREATE ASSERTION
command in the following example uses this approach in creating the assertion:

Example 102: Create assertion A1 described above.

```
CREATE ASSERTION A1 CHECK
     ( NOT EXISTS (SELECT *
                        FROM PACKAGE
                        WHERE PACKCOST <
                              (SELECT MAX(SOFTCOST)
                                    FROM SOFTWARE
                                    WHERE PACKAGE.PACKID =
                                          SOFTWARE.PACKID) ) )
```

If an assertion is no longer appropriate, it can be removed by the DROP
ASSERTION command, which has the form

```
DROP ASSERTION assertion-name
```

To remove the previous assertion, for example, the command would be

```
DROP ASSERTION A1
```

The other new integrity feature relates to foreign keys. Recall that the Integrity Enhancement Feature (IEF) allows foreign keys to be specified as in the
following example:

```
CREATE TABLE PC
     ( TAGNUM      CHAR(5),
       COMPID      CHAR(4),
       EMPNUM      DECIMAL(3),
       LOCATION    CHAR(12)
       CHECK (PC.LOCATION IN ('Accounting', 'Sales',
            'Info Systems', 'Home') )
```

```
PRIMARY KEY (TAGNUM)
FOREIGN KEY (COMPID) REFERENCES COMPUTER
FOREIGN KEY (EMPNUM) REFERENCES EMPLOYEE )
```

This CREATE TABLE command indicates that *COMPID* is a foreign key that references the *COMPUTER* table and *EMPNUM* is a foreign key that references the *EMPLOYEE* table. This indicates that the value in *COMPID* must match the value for *COMPID* in some row in the *COMPUTER* table, and the value in *EMP-NUM* must match the value for *EMPNUM* in some row in the *EMPLOYEE* table.

We need to address other problems, however. One set of problems deals with updating the primary key of the referenced table, and the other concerns deleting a record in the referenced table.

The update problems occur when updating an employee's number in the *EMPLOYEE* table. If the employee is not currently assigned a PC, there is no problem. If there is a row in the *PC* table indicating that the PC is assigned to employee 124, however, and we decide to change the employee number of employee 124 to 150, how does that affect the PC? Do we even permit the operation? The answer, of course, depends on the circumstances. It relies on the policies of the organization for which we are designing the database. The possible answers to the question are summarized below:

a. One possibility is to forbid this change. In this case, we would say that *update is restricted*. The corresponding option in SQL2 is NO ACTION. The complete clause would be ON UPDATE NO ACTION.

b. A second possibility is to allow the update but indicate that the *EMPNUM* for any PC assigned to the employee must be changed to the new employee number. In this case, we would say that *update cascades*. The corresponding clause is ON UPDATE CASCADE.

c. The third, far less common, possibility would be to allow the update but change the employee number to null for those PCs assigned to the employee (provided, of course, that nulls were even allowed). In this case, we would say that *update nullifies*. The corresponding clause is ON UPDATE SET NULL.

The deletion problems occur when deleting an employee to whom a PC is currently assigned. (If no PCs are currently assigned to the employee, there is no problem.) If there is a row in the PC table indicating that the PC is assigned to employee 124, and we decide to delete employee 124, what do we do about the PC? Do we even permit the operation? The answer, as in the case of update, depends on the policies of the organization for which we are designing the database. The possible answers to the question are summarized below:

a. One possibility is to forbid the operation. In this case, we would say that *delete is restricted*. The corresponding clause is ON DELETE NO ACTION.

b. A second possibility is to allow the deletion and also to delete any PC assigned to this employee. In this case, we would say that *delete cascades*. The corresponding clause is ON DELETE NO ACTION.

   c. The third possibility, again, not nearly as common as the other two, would be to allow the deletion. But the employee number for those PCs assigned to the employee would be changed to null (provided, of course, that nulls were even allowed). In this case, we would say that *delete nullifies*. The corresponding clause is ON DELETE SET NULL.

To indicate the correct action for update or deletion, place the appropriate clause at the end of the foreign key clause. To indicate, for example, that delete is restricted (NO ACTION) and update cascades for the EMPNUM foreign key, the clause would be:

```
FOREIGN KEY (EMPNUM) REFERENCES EMPLOYEE
                ON DELETE NO ACTION
                ON UPDATE CASCADE
```

Example 103: Incorporate these foreign key options into the CREATE TABLE statement.

The complete CREATE TABLE statement, including the foreign key clauses would be:

```
CREATE TABLE PC
      ( TAGNUM      CHAR(5),
        COMPID      CHAR(4),
        EMPNUM      DECIMAL(3),
        LOCATION    CHAR(12)
        CHECK (PC.LOCATION IN ('Accounting', 'Sales',
             'Info Systems', 'Home') )
        PRIMARY KEY (TAGNUM)
        FOREIGN KEY (COMPID) REFERENCES COMPUTER
        FOREIGN KEY (EMPNUM) REFERENCES EMPLOYEE
                       ON DELETE NO ACTION
                       ON UPDATE CASCADE )
```

Incidentally, NO ACTION is the default, so you do not need to include ON DELETE NO ACTION or ON UPDATE NO ACTION.

USING SQLSTATE

SQLCODE not totally standardized. Each vendor could assign meanings to some of the values. In order to fix these problems without creating problems for existing systems that used the special values, SQL2 includes a second [parameter], SQLSTATE that is standardized; that is, its values are totally specified within SQL2.

SQLSTATE is used in the same fashion as SQLCODE, that is, the value in SQLSTATE is tested to determine whether the most recent SQL command was successful or not. If unsuccessful, the value will indicate what type of problem occurred.

SQLSTATE contains a five-character value. The first two characters give the class value, which indicates the general type of error. The following table lists some of the common class values and their meanings. (For a complete list, consult the SQL reference manual.)

SQLSTATE

Class Value	Meaning
00	command was successful
01	warning
02	not found
08	connection error
0A	feature not supported
21	cardinality violation
22	data exception
23	constraint violation
24	invalid cursor state
25	invalid transaction state
28	invalid authID specification
2B	dependent privileges exist
2D	invalid transaction termination
34	invalid cursor name
3C	ambiguous cursor name
3D	invalid catalog name
3F	invalid schema name
40	rollback
42	syntax or access error
44	check option violation

The final three characters give the subclass value, a value that further refines the meaning of the error. For example, if the class value is 22 (data exception), a subclass value of 012 indicates division by zero, whereas a subclass value of 003 indicates a numeric value that was out of range. (Again, for a complete list, consult the SQL reference manual.)

SUMMARY

Following is a summary of the material covered in Chapter 8:

1. To indicate that the commands for a logical transaction should be made permanent, use the COMMIT command.
2. To indicate that the commands for a logical transaction should be undone, use the ROLLBACK command.
3. To include options within a SELECT statement or UPDATE statement, use the CASE clause.
4. To specify a domain, use the CREATE DOMAIN command.
5. To use a domain in a CREATE TABLE command, use the name of the domain in place of a data type.
6. To perform a natural join, use the NATURAL JOIN clause.
7. To perform a left, right, or full outer join, use the LEFT OUTER, RIGHT OUTER, or FULL OUTER clause.
8. To perform an intersection, use the INTERSECT operator.
9. To perform a difference, use the EXCEPT operator.
10. To create an assertion, use the CREATE ASSERTION command.
11. To specify rules for foreign keys, use the ON DELETE and ON UPDATE clauses.
12. SQLSTATE is a new parameter designed to overcome some of the problems associated with SQLCODE.

EXERCISE (Chazy Associates)

1. Describe the purpose of COMMIT and ROLLBACK.
2. Write an SQL query to list the tag number, computer ID, employee number, and location code for each PC. The location code is 1 if the location is "Accounting," 2 if the location is "Home," 3 if the location is "Info Systems," and 4 if it is "Sales."
3. Create a domain called *PACKTYPES*. (Legal values are Accounting, Database, Spreadsheet, and Word Processing.) Once you have created the domain, use it in a CREATE TABLE command for the *PACKAGE* table.
4. Give the command to perform a natural join of the *PC* and *SOFTWARE* tables. Give the command to perform left outer, right outer, and full outer joins of the same two tables. What is the difference in these joins?
5. Use the INTERSECT command to list the tag numbers and computer IDs of any PCs assigned to Ramon Alvarez that have a database package installed on them.
6. Use the EXCEPT command to list the tag numbers and computer IDs of any PCs assigned to Ramon Alvarez that do not have a database package installed on them.
7. Create an assertion for the *PC* table to make sure no employee is assigned

more than three PCs. (*Hint:* How would you find the employees who are assigned more than three PCs?)

8. No package that has related software records may be deleted. The package ID of a package with related software records may be changed, provided the package ID on all related records is changed as well. Give the appropriate specifications for the foreign key.

9. What problems with SQLCODE are addressed by SQLSTATE?

EXERCISES (Movies)

1. Describe the purpose of COMMIT and ROLLBACK.
2. Write an SQL query to list the movie number, movie title, movie type, and critics' evaluation for each movie. The critics' evaluation is EXCELLENT if the value in the *CRIT* field is 4, VERY GOOD if it is 3, GOOD if it is 2, FAIR if it is 1, and POOR if it is 0.
3. Create a domain called *MVTYPES*. Legal values are COMEDY, DRAMA, HORROR, RELIGI, SUSPEN, and WESTER. One you have done so, use this domain in a CREATE TABLE command for the *MOVIE* table.
4. Give the command to perform a natural join of the *MEMBER* and *TAPE* tables. Give the command to perform left outer, right outer, and full outer joins of the same two tables. What is the difference in these joins?
5. Use the INTERSECT command to list the tape number and movie number for all tapes on which the movie is a comedy or that is rented by Mark Peterson.
6. Use the EXCEPT command to list the tape number and movie number for all tapes on which the movie is a comedy but are currently rented by someone other than Mark Peterson.
7. Create an assertion for the *MOVSTAR* table to make sure no star appears in more than eight movies. (*Hint:* How would you find the stars who appeared in more than eight movies?)
8. No director that has related movie records may be deleted. The director number of a director with related movie records may be changed, provided the director number on all related records is changed as well. Give the appropriate specifications for the foreign key.
9. What problems with SQLCODE are addressed by SQLSTATE?

List of Examples

Example 1: Describe the layout of the package table to the DBMS.

```
CREATE TABLE PACKAGE
    (PACKID          CHAR(4),
     PACKNAME        CHAR(20),
     PACKVER         DECIMAL(3,2),
     PACKTYPE        CHAR(15),
     PACKCOST        DECIMAL(5,2))
```

Example 2: Add the employee (124, 'Alvarez, Ramon', 1212) to the database.

```
INSERT INTO EMPLOYEE
     VALUES
     (124,'Alvarez, Ramon',1212)
```

Example 3: Add the second and third employees (567, 'Feinstein, Betty', 8716) and (611, 'Dinh, Melissa', 2963) to the database.

```
INSERT INTO EMPLOYEE
     VALUES
     (567,'Feinstein, Betty',8716)
INSERT INTO EMPLOYEE
     VALUES
     (611,'Dinh, Melissa',2963)
```

Example 4: Suppose that when adding data for employee 611, Melissa Dinh, as shown in Example 3, we didn't know her phone number. The number should therefore be set to null.

```
INSERT INTO EMPLOYEE (EMPNUM, EMPNAME)
     VALUES
     (611,'Dinh, Melissa')
```

147

Example 5: List the ID, name, and cost of all software packages in the database.

```
SELECT PACKID, PACKNAME, PACKCOST
    FROM PACKAGE
```

Example 6: List the complete PC table.

```
SELECT *
    FROM PC
```

Example 7: What is the name of employee 124?

```
SELECT EMPNAME
    FROM EMPLOYEE
    WHERE EMPNUM = 124
```

Example 8: Find the package ID and name for any package whose type is Database.

```
SELECT PACKID, PACKNAME
    FROM PACKAGE
    WHERE PACKTYPE = 'Database'
```

Example 9: List the IDs and names of all packages whose type is Database and whose cost is over $400.

```
SELECT PACKID, PACKNAME
    FROM PACKAGE
    WHERE PACKTYPE = 'Database'
    AND PACKCOST > 400
```

Example 10: List the names of all packages whose type is Database or whose cost is over $400.

```
SELECT PACKNAME
    FROM PACKAGE
    WHERE PACKTYPE = 'Database'
    OR PACKCOST > 400
```

Example 11: List the names of all packages that are not of type Database.

```
SELECT PACKNAME
    FROM PACKAGE
    WHERE NOT (PACKTYPE = 'Database')
```

Example 12: List the ID, name, and cost of all packages whose cost is between $200 and $400.

```
SELECT PACKID, PACKNAME, PACKCOST
    FROM EMPLOYEE
    WHERE PACKCOST BETWEEN 200 AND 400
```

Example 13: Suppose the packages in the database are all to be discounted 10%. List the ID, name, and discounted cost for all packages.

```
SELECT PACKID, PACKNAME, (.90 * PACKCOST)
    FROM PACKAGE
```

Example 14: Suppose the packages in the database are all to be discounted 10%. List the ID, name, and discounted cost for all packages whose discounted price is at most $200.

```
SELECT PACKID, PACKNAME, (.90 * PACKCOST)
    FROM PACKAGE
    WHERE (.90 * PACKCOST) <= 200
```

Example 15: List the ID and name of all packages whose name contains an ampersand (&).

```
SELECT PACKID, PACKNAME
    FROM PACKAGE
    WHERE PACKNAME LIKE '%&%'
```

Example 16: List the ID, name, and type of all packages whose type is Database, Spreadsheet, or Word Processing.

```
SELECT PACKID, PACKNAME, PACKTYPE
    FROM PACKAGE
    WHERE PACKTYPE IN ('Database', 'Spreadsheet',
    'Word Processing')
```

Example 17: List the number, name, and phone of all employees. Order the output by name.

```
SELECT EMPNUM, EMPNAME, EMPPHONE
    FROM EMPLOYEE
    ORDER BY EMPNAME
```

Example 18: List the package ID, name, type, and cost. The output should be sorted by package type. Within a group of packages of the same type, the output is to be sorted by decreasing cost.

```
SELECT PACKID, PACKNAME, PACKTYPE, PACKCOST
    FROM PACKAGE
    ORDER BY PACKTYPE, PACKCOST DESC
```

Example 19: How many packages are of type Database?

```
SELECT COUNT(*)
    FROM PACKAGE
    WHERE PACKTYPE = 'Database'
```

Example 20: Find the number of packages and the total of their costs.

```
SELECT COUNT(PACKID), SUM(PACKCOST)
    FROM PACKAGE
```

Example 21: Find the employee numbers of all employees who are currently assigned PCs.

```
SELECT EMPNUM
    FROM PC
```

Example 22: Find the numbers of all employees who are currently assigned PCs. List each employee number exactly once.

```
SELECT DISTINCT EMPNUM
    FROM PC
```

Example 23: Count the number of employees who are currently assigned PCs.

```
SELECT COUNT(DISTINCT EMPNUM)
    FROM PC
```

Example 24: List the package ID and name for all packages whose cost is greater than the average cost of the database packages.

```
SELECT PACKID, PACKNAME
    FROM PACKAGE
    WHERE PACKCOST >
            (SELECT AVG(PACKCOST)
                FROM PACKAGE
                WHERE PACKTYPE = 'Database')
```

Example 25: For each PC, list the tag number along with the total value of the software installed on the PC.

```
SELECT SUM(SOFTCOST)
    FROM SOFTWARE
    WHERE TAGNUM = 32808
```

Example 26: List the tag number and the total value of software for each PC on which the value of the software is more than $600.

```
SELECT TAGNUM, SUM(SOFTCOST)
    FROM SOFTWARE
    GROUP BY TAGNUM
    HAVING SUM(SOFTCOST) > 600
    ORDER BY TAGNUM
```

Example 27: List each package type together with the number of packages of that type.

```
SELECT PACKTYPE, COUNT(PACKID)
    FROM PACKAGE
    GROUP BY PACKTYPE
```

Example 28: Repeat Example 27, but only list those types for which there are more than one package.

```
SELECT PACKTYPE, COUNT(PACKID)
    FROM PACKAGE
    GROUP BY PACKTYPE
    HAVING COUNT(PACKID) > 1
```

Example 29: List each package type together with the number of packages of that type that cost more than $150.

```
SELECT PACKTYPE, COUNT(PACKID)
    FROM PACKAGE
    WHERE PACKCOST > 150
    GROUP BY PACKTYPE
```

Example 30: Repeat Example 29, but only list those types for which there are more than one package.

```
SELECT PACKTYPE, COUNT(PACKID)
    FROM PACKAGE
    WHERE PACKCOST > 150
    GROUP BY PACKTYPE
    HAVING COUNT(PACKID) > 1
```

Example 31: List the number and name of all employees whose phone number is null (unknown).

```
SELECT EMPNUM, EMPNAME
    FROM EMPLOYEE
    WHERE EMPPHONE IS NULL
```

Example 32: For each PC, list the tag number and computer ID together with the number and name of the employee to whom the PC has been assigned.

```
SELECT TAGNUM, COMPID, EMPLOYEE.EMPNUM, EMPNAME
    FROM PC, EMPLOYEE
    WHERE PC.EMPNUM = EMPLOYEE.EMPNUM
```

Example 33: For each PC whose location is "Home," list the tag number and computer ID together with the number and name of the employee to whom the PC has been assigned.

```
SELECT TAGNUM, COMPID, EMPLOYEE.EMPNUM, EMPNAME
    FROM PC, EMPLOYEE
    WHERE PC.EMPNUM = EMPLOYEE.EMPNUM
    AND LOCATION = 'Home'
```

Example 34: For each package that has been installed on a PC, find the tag number of the PC, the package ID, the package name, the installation date, the software cost, and the package cost.

```
SELECT TAGNUM, SOFTWARE.PACKID, PACKNAME, INSTDATE,
        SOFTCOST, PACKCOST
    FROM SOFTWARE, PACKAGE
    WHERE SOFTWARE.PACKID = PACKAGE.PACKID
```

Example 35: Find the names of all packages installed on the PC with tag number 32808.

```
SELECT PACKNAME
    FROM SOFTWARE, PACKAGE
    WHERE SOFTWARE.PACKID = PACKAGE.PACKID
    AND TAGNUM = '32808'
```

Example 36: Find the tag number and computer ID of all PCs on which package WP08 has been installed.

```
SELECT TAGNUM, COMPID
    FROM PC
    WHERE TAGNUM IN
            (SELECT TAGNUM
                FROM SOFTWARE
                WHERE PACKID = 'WP08')
```

Example 37: Find the tag number and computer ID of all PCs on which a package whose type is Database has been installed.

```
SELECT TAGNUM, COMPID
    FROM PC
    WHERE TAGNUM IN
            (SELECT TAGNUM
```

```
        FROM SOFTWARE
        WHERE PACKID IN
              (SELECT PACKID
                    FROM PACKAGE
                    WHERE PACKTYPE = 'Database'))
```

Example 38: List the tag number, the computer ID, the employee number, and the total value of installed software for all PCs on which the total value is over $100. Order the results by tag number.

```
SELECT PC.TAGNUM, COMPID, EMPNUM, SUM(SOFTCOST)
    FROM PC, SOFTWARE
    WHERE PC.TAGNUM = SOFTWARE.TAGNUM
    GROUP BY PC.TAGNUM, COMPID, EMPNUM
    HAVING SUM(SOFTCOST) > 100
    ORDER BY PC.TAGNUM
```

Example 39: For each PC, list the tag number and computer ID together with the number and name of the employee to whom the PC has been assigned.

```
SELECT TAGNUM, COMPID, E.EMPNUM, EMPNAME
    FROM PC P, EMPLOYEE E
    WHERE P.EMPNUM = E.EMPNUM
```

Example 40: Find any pairs of packages that have the same name.

```
SELECT FIRST.PACKID, FIRST.PACKNAME, SECOND.PACKID,
    SECOND.PACKNAME
    FROM PACKAGE FIRST, PACKAGE SECOND
    WHERE FIRST.PACKNAME = SECOND.PACKNAME
    AND FIRST.PACKID < SECOND.PACKID
```

Example 41: For each installed package, list the package ID, the package name, the installation date, the tag number of the PC on which it was installed, the computer ID of the PC, the number of the employee to whom the PC is assigned, and the name of the employee.

```
SELECT SOFTWARE.PACKID, PACKNAME, INSTDATE, SOFTWARE.TAGNUM,
    COMPUTER.COMPID, PC.EMPNUM, EMPNAME
    FROM SOFTWARE, PACKAGE, PC, EMPLOYEE
    WHERE PACKAGE.PACKID = SOFTWARE.PACKID
    AND    PC.TAGNUM = SOFTWARE.TAGNUM
    AND    EMPLOYEE.EMPNUM = PC.EMPNUM
```

Example 42: List the computer ID and manufacturer's name of all computers that either have a 486DX processor or have been assigned for home use, or both.

```
SELECT COMPID, MFGNAME
    FROM COMPUTER
    WHERE PROCTYPE = '486DX'
UNION
SELECT COMPUTER.COMPID, MFGNAME
    FROM COMPUTER, PC
    WHERE COMPUTER.COMPID = PC.COMPID
    AND LOCATION = 'Home'
```

Example 43: List the computer ID and manufacturer's name of all computers that have a 486DX processor and have been assigned for home use.

```
SELECT COMPID, MFGNAME
    FROM COMPUTER
    WHERE PROCTYPE = '486DX'
    AND COMPID IN
        (SELECT COMPID
            FROM PC
            WHERE LOCATION = 'Home')
```

Example 44: List the computer ID and manufacturer's name of all computers that have a 486DX processor but have not been assigned for home use.

```
SELECT COMPID, MFGNAME
    FROM COMPUTER
    WHERE PROCTYPE = '486DX'
    AND COMPID IN
        (SELECT COMPID
            FROM PC
            WHERE LOCATION = 'Home')
```

Example 45: Find the package ID, tag number, installation date, and software cost of those software records on which the cost is larger than the package cost of every package in the *PACKAGE* table.

```
SELECT PACKID, TAGNUM, INSTDATE, SOFTCOST
    FROM SOFTWARE
    WHERE SOFTCOST > ALL
        (SELECT PACKCOST
            FROM PACKAGE)
```

Example 46: Find the package ID, tag number, installation date, and software cost of those software records on which the cost is larger than the package cost of at least one package in the *PACKAGE* table.

```
SELECT PACKID, TAGNUM, INSTDATE, SOFTCOST
    FROM SOFTWARE
    WHERE SOFTCOST > ANY
        (SELECT PACKCOST
            FROM PACKAGE)
```

Example 47: Change the name of package DB33 to 'MANTA II'.

```
UPDATE PACKAGE
    SET PACKNAME = 'MANTA II'
    WHERE PACKID = 'DB33'
```

Example 48: For each package of type Database whose cost is over $400, increase the cost by 2%.

```
UPDATE PACKAGE
    SET PACKCOST = PACKCOST * 1.02
    WHERE PACKTYPE = 'Database'
    AND PACKCOST > 400
```

Example 49: Add a new employee to the database. The employee number is 402, the name is Robert Sanders (Sanders, Robert), and the phone number is 2056.

```
INSERT INTO EMPLOYEE
    VALUES
    (402,'Sanders, Robert',2056)
```

Example 50: Delete from the database the employee whose phone number is 8716. To delete data from the database, use the DELETE command, as in the following:

```
DELETE EMPLOYEE
    WHERE EMPPHONE = 8716
```

Example 51: Create a new table called *DBPACK* containing the rows in the *PACKAGE* table of type Database.

```
CREATE TABLE DBPACK
    (PACKID      CHAR(4),
    PACKNAME    CHAR(20),
    PACKVER     DECIMAL(3,2),
    PACKTYPE    CHAR(15),
    PACKCOST    DECIMAL(5,2))

INSERT INTO DBPACK
    SELECT *
        FROM PACKAGE
        WHERE PACKTYPE = 'Database'
```

Example 52: Create a new table called *WPPACK* containing the package ID, name, and type for all rows in the *PACKAGE* table of type Word Processing. The rows should be sorted by package name.

```
CREATE TABLE DBPACK
    (PACKID        CHAR(4),
     PACKNAME      CHAR(20),
     PACKVER       DECIMAL(3,2),
     PACKCOST      DECIMAL(5,2))
INSERT INTO WPPACK
        SELECT PACKID, PACKNAME, PACKTYPE
            FROM PACKAGE
            WHERE PACKTYPE = 'Word Processing'
            ORDER BY PACKNAME
```

Example 53: Set the phone number of employee 124 to null.

```
UPDATE EMPLOYEE
      SET EMPPHONE = NULL
      WHERE EMPNUM = 124
```

Example 54: Chazy Associates decides to maintain an employee type for each employee in the database. This type is E for executive employees, A for administrative employees, P for professional employees, and H for hourly employees. Add this as a new column in the employee table.

```
ALTER TABLE EMPLOYEE
      ADD EMPTYPE        CHAR(1)
```

Example 55: We no longer need the *PACKVER* column in the *PACKAGE* table, so we should delete it.

```
ALTER TABLE PACKAGE
      DELETE PACKVER
```

Example 56: The length of the *EMPNAME* column is too short. Increase it to 30 characters.

```
ALTER TABLE EMPLOYEE
      CHANGE COLUMN EMPNAME TO CHAR(30)
```

Example 57: The *COMPUTER* table is no longer needed in the Chazy Associates database, so delete it.

```
DROP TABLE COMPUTER
```

Example 58: Define a view, *DATABASE*, that consists of the package ID, the package name, and the cost of all packages whose type is Database.

```
CREATE VIEW DATABASE AS
     SELECT PACKID, PACKNAME, PACKCOST
          FROM PACKAGE
          WHERE PACKTYPE = 'Database'
```

Example 59: Define a view, *DATABASE*, that consists of the package ID, the package name, and the cost of all packages whose type is Database. In this view, the package ID column is to be called *PKID*, the package name column is to be called *NAME*, and the package cost column is to be called *COST*.

```
CREATE VIEW DATABASE (PKID, NAME, COST) AS
     SELECT PACKID, PACKNAME, PACKCOST
          FROM PACKAGE
          WHERE PACKTYPE = 'Database'
```

Example 60: Define a view, *PCEMP*, that consists of the tag number, computer ID, employee number, and employee name for all PCs and matching employees in the *PC* and *EMPLOYEE* tables.

```
CREATE VIEW PCEMP AS
     SELECT TAGNUM, COMPID, PC.EMPNUM, EMPNAME
          FROM PC, EMPLOYEE
          WHERE PC.EMPNUM = EMPLOYEE.EMPNUM
```

Example 61: Define a view, *TYPEPACK*, that consists of a package type and the number of packages (*NUMBPACK*) that are of that type.

```
CREATE VIEW TYPEPACK (PACKTYPE, NUMBPACK) AS
     SELECT PACKTYPE, COUNT(PACKID)
          FROM PACKAGE
          GROUP BY PACKTYPE
```

Example 62: The *DATABASE* view is no longer necessary, so remove it.

```
DROP VIEW DATABASE
```

Example 63: User Jones must be able to retrieve data from the *EMPLOYEE* table.

```
GRANT SELECT ON EMPLOYEE TO JONES
```

Example 64: Users Smith and Brown must be able to add new packages.

```
GRANT INSERT ON PACKAGE TO SMITH, BROWN
```

Example 65: User Anderson must be able to change the name or phone number of employees.

```
GRANT UPDATE ON EMPLOYEE (EMPNAME, EMPPHONE) TO ANDERSON
```

Example 66: User Martin must be able to delete software records.

```
GRANT DELETE ON SOFTWARE TO MARTIN
```

Example 67: All users must be able to retrieve package IDs, names, and types.

```
GRANT SELECT ON PACKAGE (PACKID, PACKNAME, PACKTYPE)
      TO PUBLIC
```

Example 68: User Roberts must be able to create an index on the *COMPUTER* table.

```
GRANT INDEX ON COMPUTER TO ROBERTS
```

Example 69: User Thomas must be able to change the structure of the *EMPLOYEE* table.

```
GRANT ALTER ON EMPLOYEE TO THOMAS
```

Example 70: User Wilson must have all privileges on the *COMPUTER*, *EMPLOYEE*, and *PC* tables.

```
GRANT ALL ON COMPUTER, EMPLOYEE, PC TO WILSON
```

Example 71: User Jones is no longer allowed to retrieve data from the *EMPLOYEE* table.

```
REVOKE SELECT ON EMPLOYEE FROM JONES
```

Example 72: Permit Marilyn Johnson, the database specialist at Chazy Associates, to access any data concerning packages of type Database, but do not allow her to access data concerning any other packages.

```
CREATE VIEW DBPACK AS
      SELECT *
          FROM PACKAGE
          WHERE PACKID = 'Database'
GRANT SELECT ON DBPACK TO MARILYN JOHNSON
```

Example 73: Create a unique index on the *PACKID* column within the *PACKAGE* table. The index is to be called *PACKIND*.

```
CREATE UNIQUE INDEX PACKIND ON PACKAGE (PACKID)
```

Example 74: Create an index called *CUSTIND2* on the *COMPID* column within the *EMPLOYEE* table.

```
CREATE INDEX CUSTIND2 ON EMPLOYEE (COMPID)
```

Example 75: Create a unique index called *SOFTIND* on the *PACKID, TAGNUM* combination, which is the primary key of the *SOFTWARE* table.

```
CREATE UNIQUE INDEX SOFTIND
          ON SOFTWARE (PACKID, TAGNUM)
```

Example 76: Create an index for the *PACKAGE* table, called *PACKIND3* on the combination of package name and descending package version (that is, the latest version will be listed first).

```
CREATE INDEX PACKIND3 ON PACKAGE (PACKNAME, PACKVER DESC)
```

Example 77: Delete the index called *PACKIND*.

```
DROP INDEX PACKIND
```

Example 78: List the name and creator of all tables known to the system.

```
SELECT NAME, CREATOR
    FROM SYSTABLES
```

Example 79: List all the columns in the *PACKAGE* table as well as their associated data types.

```
SELECT COLNAME, COLTYPE
    FROM SYSCOLUMNS
    WHERE TBNAME = 'PACKAGE'
```

Example 80: List all tables that contain a column called *EMPNUM*.

```
SELECT TBNAME
    FROM SYSCOLUMNS
    WHERE COLNAME = 'EMPNUM'
```

Example 81: Create the *PC* table for the Chazy Associates database. Valid locations are to be "Accounting," "Sales," "Info Systems," and "Home." The primary key is to be *TAGNUM*. *COMPID* is a foreign key that is required to match the primary key of the *COMPUTER* table, and *EMPNUM* is a foreign key that is required to match the primary key of the *EMPLOYEE* table.

```
CREATE TABLE PC
     ( TAGNUM        CHAR(5),
       COMPID        CHAR(4),
       EMPNUM        DECIMAL(3),
       LOCATION      CHAR(12)
       CHECK (PC.LOCATION IN ('Accounting', 'Sales',
            'Info Systems', 'Home') )
       PRIMARY KEY (TAGNUM)
       FOREIGN KEY (COMPID) REFERENCES COMPUTER
       FOREIGN KEY (EMPNUM) REFERENCES EMPLOYEE )
```

Example 82: Obtain the name of package SS11 and place it in *W-PACKNAME*.

```
EXEC SQL
     SELECT PACKNAME
          INTO :W-PACKNAME
          FROM PACKAGE
          WHERE PACKID = 'SS11'
END-EXEC.
```

Example 83: Obtain all information about the package whose ID is stored in the host variable *W-PACKID*.

```
EXEC SQL
     SELECT PACKNAME, PACKVER, PACKTYPE, PACKCOST
          INTO :W-PACKNAME, :W-PACKVER, :W-PACKTYPE,
               :W-PACKCOST
          FROM PACKAGE
          WHERE PACKID = :W-PACKID
END-EXEC.
```

Example 84: Obtain the tag number and computer ID of the PC whose tag number is stored in the host variable W-TAGNUM as well as the number and name of the employee to whom the PC is assigned.

```
EXEC SQL
     SELECT COMPID, EMPLOYEE.EMPNUM, EMPNAME
          INTO :W-COMPID, :W-EMPNUM, :W-EMPNAME
          FROM PC, EMPLOYEE
          WHERE PC.EMPNUM = EMPLOYEE.EMPNUM
          AND PC.TAGNUM = :W-TAGNUM
END-EXEC.
```

Example 85: Add a row to the package table. The package ID, name, version, type, and cost have already been placed in the variables *W-PACKID*, *W-PACKNAME, W-PACKVER, W-PACKTYPE,* and *W-PACKCOST*, respectively.

```
EXEC SQL
    INSERT
        INTO PACKAGE
        VALUES (:W-PACKID, :W-PACKNAME, :W-PACKVER,
            :W-PACKTYPE, :W-PACKCOST)
END-EXEC.
```

Example 86: Change the name of the package whose ID is currently stored in *W-PACKID* to the value currently stored in *W-PACKNAME*.

```
EXEC SQL
    UPDATE PACKAGE
        SET PACKNAME = :W-PACKNAME
        WHERE PACKID = :W-PACKID
END-EXEC.
```

Example 87: Add the amount stored in the host variable *INCREASE-IN-COST* to the package cost of all packages of type Database.

```
EXEC SQL
    UPDATE PACKAGE
        SET PACKCOST = PACKCOST + :INCREASE-IN-COST
        WHERE PACKTYPE = 'Database'
END-EXEC.
```

Example 88: Delete the computer whose ID is currently stored in *W-COMPID* from the *COMPUTER* table.

```
EXEC SQL
    DELETE
        FROM COMPUTER
        WHERE COMPID = :W-COMPID
END-EXEC.
```

Example 89: Delete from the *SOFTWARE* table all records for the PC whose tag number is currently stored in the host variable *W-TAGNUM*.

```
EXEC SQL
    DELETE
        FROM SOFTWARE
        WHERE TAGNUM = :W-TAGNUM
END-EXEC.
```

Example 90: Retrieve the computer ID and manufacturer's name of all computers whose processor type is stored in the host variable *W-PROCTYPE*. (Program uses the following commands.)

```
EXEC SQL
    DECLARE COMPGROUP CURSOR FOR
        SELECT COMPID, MFGNAME
            FROM COMPUTER
            WHERE PROCTYPE = :W-PROCTYPE
END-EXEC.
EXEC SQL
    OPEN COMPGROUP
END-EXEC.
EXEC SQL
    FETCH COMPGROUP
        INTO :W-COMPID, :W-MFGNAME
END-EXEC.
EXEC SQL
    CLOSE COMPGROUP
END-EXEC.
```

Example 91: For each installation of the package whose ID is stored in *W-PACKID*, list the package ID, the package name, the installation date, the tag number of the PC on which it was installed, the computer ID of the PC, the number of the employee to whom the PC is assigned, and the name of the employee. Sort the results by employee number.

```
EXEC SQL
    DECLARE ORDGROUP CURSOR FOR
        SELECT SOFTWARE.PACKID, PACKNAME, INSTDATE,
            SOFTWARE.TAGNUM, COMPUTER.COMPID, PC.EMPNUM, EMPNAME
            FROM SOFTWARE, PACKAGE, PC, EMPLOYEE
            WHERE PACKAGE.PACKID = :W-PACKID
            AND   PACKAGE.PACKID = SOFTWARE.PACKID
            AND   PC.TAGNUM = SOFTWARE.TAGNUM
            AND   EMPLOYEE.EMPNUM = PC.EMPNUM
            ORDER BY EMPLOYEE.EMPNUM
END-EXEC.
```

Example 92: Subtract 5% from the package cost of each package whose package name is stored in W-PACKNAME and for which there are three or more installations at Chazy. Subtract 2% from the package cost for all such packages with two installations. Write the ID and name of all such packages for which there is only one installation.

```
EXEC SQL
   DECLARE PACKGROUP CURSOR FOR
      SELECT PACKID, PACKNAME, PACKCOST, NUMINST
            FROM PACKAGE
            WHERE PACKNAME = :W-PACKNAME
            FOR UPDATE OF PACKCOST
END-EXEC.
```

Example 93: List the package ID and package name of all packages. You also want to list the word "HIGH" if the package cost is over $400; "MEDIUM" if the package cost is more than $200, but less than $400; "LOW" if the cost is more than $100, but less than $200; or "VERY LOW" if the cost is less than $100. To do so, you could use the following SELECT command:

```
SELECT PACKID, PACKNAME,
      CASE
         WHEN PACKCOST >= 400 THEN 'HIGH'
         WHEN PACKCOST >= 200 AND PACKCOST < 400 THEN 'MEDIUM'
         WHEN PACKCOST >= 100 AND PACKCOST < 200 THEN 'LOW'
         ELSE 'VERY LOW'
      END
      FROM PACKAGE
```

Example 94: Assume that there is an additional column in the *PACKAGE* table, *NUMINST*, that indicates the number of units of the package that are currently installed. Subtract 5% from the package cost of each package for which there are three or more installations at Chazy. Subtract 2% from the package cost for packages with two installations. Subtract 1% from the package cost for all other packages.

```
UPDATE PACKAGE
      SET PACKCOST = CASE
         WHEN NUMINST >= 3 THEN PACKCOST = .95 * PACKCOST
         WHEN NUMINST = 2 THEN PACKCOST = .98 * PACKCOST
         ELSE PACKCOST = .99 * PACKCOST
```

Example 95: Create the LOCATIONS domain.

```
CREATE DOMAIN LOCATIONS CHAR(12)
      CHECK (VALUE = 'Accounting' OR VALUE = 'Sales' OR
            VALUE = 'Info Systems' OR VALUE = 'Home')
```

Example 96: Use SQL2 commands to join the tables.

```
SELECT TAGNUM, COMPID, EMPNUM, EMPNAME
      FROM PC NATURAL JOIN EMPLOYEE
```

Example 97: Perform a left outer join in SQL2.

```
SELECT TAGNUM, COMPID, EMPNUM, EMPNAME
    FROM PC LEFT OUTER JOIN EMPLOYEE
```

Example 98: Perform a right outer join in SQL2.

```
SELECT TAGNUM, COMPID, EMPNUM, EMPNAME
    FROM PC RIGHT OUTER JOIN EMPLOYEE
```

Example 99: Perform a full outer join in SQL2.

```
SELECT TAGNUM, COMPID, EMPNUM, EMPNAME
    FROM PC FULL OUTER JOIN EMPLOYEE
```

Example 100: Perform an intersection in SQL2.

```
SELECT COMPID, MFGNAME
    FROM COMPUTER
    WHERE PROCTYPE = '486DX'
INTERSECT
SELECT COMPUTER.COMPID, MFGNAME
    FROM COMPUTER, PC
    WHERE COMPUTER.COMPID = PC.COMPID
    AND LOCATION = 'Home'
```

Example 101: Perform a difference in SQL2.

```
SELECT COMPID, MFGNAME
    FROM COMPUTER
    WHERE PROCTYPE = '486DX'
EXCEPT
SELECT COMPUTER.COMPID, MFGNAME
    FROM COMPUTER, PC
    WHERE COMPUTER.COMPID = PC.COMPID
    AND LOCATION = 'Home'
```

Example 102: Create assertion A1 described above.

```
CREATE ASSERTION A1 CHECK
    ( NOT EXISTS (SELECT *
                    FROM PACKAGE
                    WHERE PACKCOST <
                        (SELECT MAX(SOFTCOST)
                            FROM SOFTWARE
                            WHERE PACKAGE.PACKID =
                                SOFTWARE.PACKID) ) )
```

Example 103: Incorporate foreign key options into a CREATE TABLE statement.

```
CREATE TABLE PC
     ( TAGNUM       CHAR(5),
       COMPID       CHAR(4),
       EMPNUM       DECIMAL(3),
       LOCATION     CHAR(12)
       CHECK (PC.LOCATION IN ('Accounting', 'Sales',
            'Info Systems', 'Home') )
       PRIMARY KEY (TAGNUM)
       FOREIGN KEY (COMPID) REFERENCES COMPUTER
       FOREIGN KEY (EMPNUM) REFERENCES EMPLOYEE
                         ON DELETE NO ACTION
                         ON UPDATE CASCADE )
```

Answers to Odd-Numbered Exercises

EXERCISES CHAZY ASSOCIATES

CHAPTER 1

1. 48X
    D1.
3. B121, 48X
    B221, 48D
    C007, D1.
5. DB32, Manta
    DB33, Manta
    SS11, Limitless View.
7. AC01, Boise Accounting, 3.00, 653.23.
9. 567, Betty Feinstein.
11. AC01, Boise Accounting, 3.00, Accounting, 725.83
    DB33, Manta, 2.10, Database, 430.18
    DB32, Manta, 1.50, Database, 380.00
    SS11, Limitless View, 5.30 Spreadsheet, 217.95
    WP08, Words & More, 2.00, Word Processing, 185.00
    WP09, Freeware Processing, 4.27, Word Processing, 30.00
13. 107.50
15. Accounting, 725.83
    Database, 405.09
    Spreadsheet, 217.95
    Word Processing, 107.50
    Database, 405.09
    Word Processing, 107.50

17. 37691, B121, Bantam
    59836, B221, Bantam
19. 124, Alvarez, Ramon
    567, Feinstein, Betty
21. 32808, M759, Boise Accounting, 3.00, Accounting
    32808, M759, Manta, 1.50, Database
    37691, B121, Manta, 1.50, Database
    57772, C007, Manta, 2.10, Database
    37691, B121, Words & More, 2.00, Word Processing
    57772, C007, Words & More, 2.00, Word Processing
    59836, B221, Freeware Processing, 4.27, Word Processing
    77740, M759, Freeware Processing, 4.27, Word Processing
23. 32808, M759
    37691, B121
    57772, C007
25. 37691, B121
27. 32808, M759
    37691, B121
    57772, C007
    59836, B221

CHAPTER 2

```
1. CREATE TABLE PACKAGE
        (PACKID          CHAR(4),
         PACKNAME        CHAR(20),
         PACKVER         DECIMAL(3,2),
         PACKTYPE        CHAR(15),
         PACKCOST        DECIMAL(5,2))

   CREATE TABLE COMPUTER
        (COMPID     DECIMAL(2),
         MFGNAME         CHAR(15),
         MFGMODEL        CHAR(25),
         PROCTYPE        DECIMAL(7,2))
```

CHAPTER 3

```
1. SELECT EMPNUM, EMPNAME
        FROM EMPLOYEE
3. SELECT MFGMODEL
        FROM COMPUTER
        WHERE PROCTYPE = '486DX'
```

5. ```
SELECT COMPID, MFGMODEL
     FROM COMPUTER
     WHERE PROCTYPE = '486DX'
     OR PROCTYPE = '486DX2'
```

7. ```
SELECT TAGNUM, PACKID
     FROM PACKAGE
     WHERE SOFTCOST > 200
     AND SOFTCOST < 500
```

or

```
SELECT TAGNUM, PACKID
     FROM PACKAGE
     WHERE SOFTCOST BETWEEN 200 AND 500
```

9. ```
SELECT TAGNUM, PACKID,   (.90 * SOFTCOST)
     FROM SOFTWARE
     WHERE .90 * SOFTCOST >= 400
```

11. ```
SELECT EMPNUM, EMPNAME
      FROM EMPLOYEE
      WHERE EMPNAME LIKE 'Feinstein%'
```

13. ```
SELECT *
      FROM PACKAGE
      ORDER BY PACKTYPE, PACKCOST DESC
```

15. ```
SELECT AVG(PACKCOST)
      FROM PACKAGE
      WHERE PACKTYPE = 'Word Processing'
```

17. ```
SELECT PACKTYPE, AVG(PACKCOST)
      FROM PACKAGE
      GROUP BY PACKTYPE
 SELECT PACKTYPE, AVG(PACKCOST)
      FROM PACKAGE
      GROUP BY PACKTYPE
      HAVING COUNT(*) > 1
```

## CHAPTER 4

1. ```
SELECT TAGNUM, PC.COMPID, MFGNAME
     FROM PC, COMPUTER
     WHERE PC.COMPID = COMPUTER.COMPID
```

3. ```
SELECT PC.TAGNUM, COMPID, SOFTWARE.PACKID,
     PACKNAME, INSTDATE
     FROM PC, SOFTWARE, PACKAGE
     WHERE PC.TAGNUM = SOFTWARE.TAGNUM
     AND SOFTWARE.PACKID = PACKAGE.PACKID
```

5. ```
SELECT EMPNUM, EMPNAME
     FROM EMPLOYEE
     WHERE EMPNUM NOT IN
          (SELECT EMPNUM
               FROM PC
               WHERE LOCATION = 'Home')
```

```
 7. SELECT MFGNAME, MFGMODEL
        FROM COMPUTER
        WHERE COMPID IN
            (SELECT COMPID
                FROM PC
                WHERE LOCATION = 'Home')
 9. SELECT F.PACKID, F.PACKNAME, S.PACKID, S.PACKNAME
        FROM PACKAGE F, PACKAGE S
        WHERE F.PACKTYPE = S.PACKTYPE
        AND F.PACKID < S.PACKID
11. SELECT TAGNUM, COMPID
        FROM PC, EMPLOYEE
        WHERE PC.EMPNUM = EMPLOYEE.EMPNUM
        AND EMPNAME = 'Alvarez, Ramon'
        AND COMPID NOT IN
            (SELECT COMPID
                FROM PC, SOFTWARE, PACKAGE
                WHERE PC.TAGNUM = SOFTWARE.TAGNUM
                AND SOFTWARE.PACKID = PACKAGE.PACKID
                AND PACKTYPE = 'Database')
13. SELECT PACKID, PACKNAME
        FROM PACKAGE
        WHERE PACKCOST > ALL
            (SELECT PACKCOST
                FROM PACKAGE
                WHERE PACKTYPE = 'Database')
```

CHAPTER 5

```
 1. UPDATE COMPUTER
        SET MFGMODEL = 'M759'
        WHERE PROCTYPE = '4GL'
 3. INSERT INTO PC
        VALUES
        ('68464', 'M759', 611, 'Home')
 5. CREATE TABLE WPPACK
        (PACKID          CHAR(4),
        PACKNAME         CHAR(20),
        PACKVER          DECIMAL(3,2),
        PACKCOST         DECIMAL(5,2))
    INSERT INTO WPPACK
        SELECT PACKID, PACKNAME, PACKVER, PACKCOST
            FROM PACKAGE
            WHERE PACKTYPE = 'Word Processing'
 7. ALTER TABLE PACKAGE
        ADD NUMINST       DECIMAL(3)
    UPDATE PACKAGE
        SET NUMINST = 0
```

```
SELECT COUNT(*)
    FROM SOFTWARE
    WHERE PACKID = 'DB32'
UPDATE PACKAGE
    SET NUMINST = (the result of previous SELECT)
        WHERE PACKID = 'DB32'
```

9. ALTER TABLE PACKAGE
      CHANGE COLUMN PACKNAME TO CHAR(30)

CHAPTER 6

1. a. CREATE VIEW SMLLPACK AS
        SELECT PACKID, PACKNAME, PACKTYPE, PACKCOST
           FROM PACKAGE
           WHERE PACKCOST <= 400

   b. SELECT PACKID, PACKNAME
        FROM SMLLPACK
        WHERE PACKTYPE = 'Database'

   c. SELECT PACKID, PACKNAME
        FROM PACKAGE
        WHERE PACKCOST <= 400
        AND PACKTYPE = 'Database'

   d. To update data using this view, PACKVER must accept nulls, since a user of the view cannot enter a package version. Other than that, there are no problems.

3. a. CREATE VIEW PCSFTCST (TAGNUM, TOTCOST) AS
        SELECT TAGNUM, SUM (SOFTCOST)
           FROM SOFTWARE
           GROUP BY TAGNUM

   b. SELECT TAGNUM, TOTCOST
        FROM PCSFTCST
        WHERE TOTCOST > 100

   c. SELECT TAGNUM, SUM(SOFTCOST)
        FROM SOFTWARE
        GROUP BY TAGNUM
        HAVING SUM(SOFTCOST) > 100

   d. It is impossible to update the database through this view since it involves statistics.

5. REVOKE SELECT ON PACKAGE FROM STILLWELL

7. DROP INDEX PACKAGEIND3

9. CREATE TABLE PACKAGE
```
        (PACKID          CHAR(4),
         PACKNAME        CHAR(20),
         PACKVER         DECIMAL(3,2),
         PACKTYPE        CHAR(15),
         PACKCOST        DECIMAL(5,2),
         CHECK (PACKAGE.PACKTYPE IN ('Accounting',
                'Database', 'Spreadsheet',
                'Accounting'))
         PRIMARY KEY (PACKID) )
```

CHAPTER 7

```
1. a. EXEC SQL
         SELECT EPMNAME, EMPPHONE
             INTO :W-EMPNAME, :W-EMPPHONE
             FROM EMPLOYEE
             WHERE EMPNUM = :W-EMPNUM
      END-EXEC
   b. EXEC SQL
         SELECT COMPID, PC.EMPNUM, EMPNAME,
                 LOCATION
             INTO :W-COMPID, :W-EMPNUM,
                 :W-EMPNAME, :W-LOCATION
             FROM PC, EMPLOYEE
             WHERE PC.EMPNUM = EMPLOYEE.EMPNUM
             AND TAGNUM = :W-TAGNUM
      END-EXEC
   c. EXEC SQL
         INSERT
             INTO PC
             VALUES (:W-TAGNUM, :W-COMPID,
                 :W-EMPNUM, :W-LOCATION)
      END-EXEC
   d. EXEC SQL
         UPDATE EMPLOYEE
             SET EMPNAME = :W-EMPNAME
             WHERE EMPNUM = :W-EMPNUM
      END-EXEC
   e. EXEC SQL
         UPDATE PACKAGE
             SET PACKCOST = PACKCOST * 1.05
             WHERE PACKTYPE = 'Database'
      END-EXEC
   f. EXEC SQL
         DELETE
             FROM EMPLOYEE
             WHERE EMPNUM = :W-EMPNUM
      END-EXEC
```

CHAPTER 8

1. COMMIT makes all the updates since the last COMMIT permanent. It also makes them available to other users. ROLLBACK reverses all the updates since the last commit.

```
3. CREATE DOMAIN PACKTYPES CHAR(15)
       CHECK (VALUE = 'Accounting' OR VALUE = 'Database' OR
           VALUE = 'Spreadsheet' OR VALUE = 'Word Processing')
```

```
CREATE TABLE PACKAGE
    (PACKID          CHAR(4),
     PACKNAME        CHAR(20),
     PACKVER         DECIMAL(3,2),
     PACKTYPE        PACKTYPES,
     PACKCOST        DECIMAL(5,2))
```

5. SELECT TAGNUM, COMPID
```
    FROM PC, EMPLOYEE
    WHERE PC.EMPNUM = EMPLOYEE.EMPNUM
    AND EMPNAME = 'Alvarez, Ramon'
INTERSECT
SELECT PC.TAGNUM, COMPID
    FROM PC, SOFTWARE, PACKAGE
    WHERE PC.TAGNUM = SOFTWARE.TAGNUM
    AND SOFTWARE.PACKID = PACKAGE.PACKID
    AND PACKTYPE = 'Database'
```

7. CREATE ASSERTION A1 CHECK
```
    ( NOT EXISTS (SELECT EMPNUM, COUNT(*)
                  FROM PC
                  GROUP BY EMPNUM
                  HAVING COUNT(*) > 3)
```

9. SQLCODE was not totally standardized. Different vendors assigned different meanings to the same value. The values of SQLSTATE, on the other hand, are specified as part of the standard.

EXERCISES MOVIES

CHAPTER 1

1.

MMBNUMB	MMBNAME	MMBADDR	MMBCTY	MMBST
1	Allen, Donna	21 Wilson	Carson	IN
2	Peterson, Mark	215 Raymond	Cedar	IN
3	Sanchez, Miquel	47 Chipwood	Mantin	IL
4	Tran, Thanh	108 College	Carson	IN
5	Roberts, Terry	602 Bridge	Hudson	MI
6	MacDonald, Greg	19 Oak	Carson	IN
7	VanderJagt, Neal	12 Bishop	Mantin	IL
8	Shippers, John	208 Grayton	Cedar	IN
9	Franklin, Trudy	103 Bedford	Brook	MI
10	Stein, Shelly	82 Harcourt	Hudson	MI

3.

DIRNUMB	DIRNAME	DIRBORN	DIRDIED
1	Allen, Woody	1935	–
2	Hitchcock, Alfred	1899	1980
3	De Mille, Cecil B.	1881	1959
4	Kramer, Stanley	1913	–
5	Kubrick, Stanley	1928	–
6	Preminger, Otto	1906	–
7	Ford, John	1895	1973

5. 11 - 17.

7. 1, Annie Hall - 2, Dr. Strangelove - 4, North by Northwest - 6, Psycho - 7, Interiors.

9. 1, Annie Hall - 2, Dr. Strangelove - 4, North by Northwest - 6, Psycho - 7, Interiors - 10, Guess Who's Coming to Dinner - 13, Judgment at Nuremberg - 18, Laura - 21, Stagecoach - 24, Grapes of Wrath.

11. 2, Mark Peterson - 6, Greg MacDonald - 7, Neal VanderJagt.

13. 2, Hitchcock, Alfred, 81 - 3, De Mille, Cecil B., 78 - 7, Ford, John, 78.

15.

MVNUMB	MVTITLE
1	Annie Hall
2	Dr. Strangelove
4	North by Northwest
5	Rope
9	Samson and Delilah
10	Guess Who's Coming to Dinner
11	Manhattan
12	Vertigo
16	Anatomy of a Murder
18	Laura
19	The Ten Commandments
20	The Moon is Blue
22	Rear Window

17.

MMBNUMB	MMBNAME	MMBADDR	MMBCTY	MMBST	JOINDATE
1	Allen, Donna	21 Wilson	Carson	IN	05/25/91
4	Tran, Thanh	108 College	Carson	IN	07/03/91
6	MacDonald, Greg	19 Oak	Carson	IN	01/29/91
2	Peterson, Mark	215 Raymond	Cedar	IN	02/20/90
8	Shippers, John	208 Grayton	Cedar	IN	09/02/91
3	Sanchez, Miquel	47 Chipwood	Mantin	IL	06/14/90
7	VanderJagt, Neal	12 Bishop	Mantin	IL	08/11/90
9	Franklin, Trudy	103 Bedford	Brook	MI	12/13/90
5	Roberts, Terry	602 Bridge	Hudson	MI	11/16/90
10	Stein, Shelly	82 Harcourt	Hudson	MI	06/21/91

19. 6.
21. 7.
23. 3, Sanchez, Miguel - 6, MacDonald, Greg - 7, VanderJagt, Neal - 9, Franklin, Trudy.
25. 1, 4 - 4, 4.
27. 1, 4 - 4, 2.
29.

TPNUMB	PURDATE	MVNUMB	MVTITLE
1	04/26/1990	1	Annie Hall
2	04/26/1990	2	Dr. Strangelove
3	04/26/1990	3	Clockwork Orange
4	04/28/1990	4	North by Northwest
5	05/12/1990	5	Rope
6	05/12/1990	6	Psycho
7	05/12/1990	7	Interiors
8	05/12/1990	8	The Birds
9	06/26/1990	6	Psycho
10	06/26/1990	9	Samson and Delilah
11	06/26/1990	10	Guess Who's Coming to Dinner
12	07/11/1990	11	Manhattan
13	08/02/1990	12	Vertigo
14	08/02/1990	6	Psycho
15	08/25/1990	13	Judgment at Nuremberg
16	08/25/1990	14	2001
17	09/07/1990	15	The Man with the Golden Arm
18	09/07/1990	16	Anatomy of a Murder
19	09/23/1990	17	Inherit the Wind
20	10/12/1990	14	2001
21	11/15/1990	18	Laura
22	11/15/1990	19	The Ten Commandments
23	12/21/1990	20	The Moon is Blue
24	01/11/1991	21	Stagecoach
25	02/14/1991	22	Rear Window
26	02/14/1991	23	Mogambo
27	03/06/1991	24	Grapes of Wrath

31.

TPNUMB	PURDATE	MVNUMB	MVTITLE
3	04/26/1990	3	Clockwork Orange
4	04/28/1990	4	North by Northwest
6	05/12/1990	6	Psycho
8	05/12/1990	8	The Birds
10	06/26/1990	9	Samson and Delilah
11	06/26/1990	10	Guess Who's Coming to Dinner
12	07/11/1990	11	Manhattan
14	08/02/1990	6	Psycho
16	08/25/1990	14	2001
17	09/07/1990	15	The Man with the Golden Arm

```
18 09/07/1990     16 Anatomy of a Murder
21 11/15/1990     18 Laura
24 01/11/1991     21 Stagecoach
```

33. 1, Allen, Woody - 4, Kramer, Stanley - 5, Kubrick, Stanley - 6, Preminger, Otto.

35.

MVTITLE	STARNAME	BRTHPLCE
Annie Hall	Allen, Woody	New York
Annie Hall	Keaton, Diane	Los Angeles
Dr. Strangelove	Sellers, Peter	Southsea, Eng.
Dr. Strangelove	Scott, George C.	Wise, Va.
Clockwork Orange	McDowell, Malcolm	Leeds, Eng.
North by Northwest	Grant, Cary	Bristol, Eng.
North by Northwest	Saint, Eva Marie	Newark, N.J.
Rope	Stewart, James	Indiana, Pa.
Psycho	Perkins, Anthony	New York
Psycho	Leigh, Janet	Merced, Cal.
Interiors	Keaton, Diane	Los Angeles
The Birds	Taylor, Rod	Sydney, Australia
The Birds	Hedren, Tippi	Lafayette, Minn.
Samson and Delilah	Mature, Victor	Louisville, Ky.
Guess Who's Coming to Dinner	Tracy, Spencer	Milwaukee
Guess Who's Coming to Dinner	Hepburn, Katharine	Hartford
Manhattan	Allen, Woody	New York
Manhattan	Keaton, Diane	Los Angeles
Vertigo	Stewart, James	Indiana, Pa.
Vertigo	Novak, Kim	Chicago
Judgment at Nuremberg	Tracy, Spencer	Milwaukee
2001	Dullea, Keir	Cleveland
The Man with the Golden Arm	Novak, Kim	Chicago
The Man with the Golden Arm	Sinatra, Frank	Hoboken, N.J.
Anatomy of a Murder	Stewart, James	Indiana, Pa.
Inherit the Wind	Tracy, Spencer	Milwaukee
Inherit the wind	March, Fredric	Racine, Wis.
Laura	Andrews, Dana	Collins, Miss.
The Ten Commandments	Heston, Charlton	Evanston, Ill.
The Moon is Blue	McNamara, Maggie	New York
The Moon is Blue	Niven, David	Kirriemuir, Scot.
Stagecoach	Wayne, John	Winterset, Iowa
Rear Window	Stewart, James	Indiana, Pa.
Rear Window	Kelly, Grace	Philadelphia
Mogambo	Gable, Clark	Cadiz, O.
Mogambo	Kelly, Grace	Philadelphia
Grapes of Wrath	Fonda, Henry	Grand Island, Neb.

37.

STARNUMB	STARNAME
6	Grant, Cary
7	Saint, Eva Marie
8	Stewart, James
9	Perkins, Anthony
10	Leigh, Janet
11	Taylor, Rod
12	Hedren, Tippi
17	Novak, Kim
26	Kelley, Grace

39.

MVTITLE	DIRNAME	STARNAME
Annie Hall	Allen, Woody	Allen, Woody
Annie Hall	Allen, Woody	Keaton, Diane
Interiors	Allen, Woody	Keaton, Diane
Manhattan	Allen, Woody	Allen, Woody
Manhattan	Allen, Woody	Keaton, Diane
North by Northwest	Hitchcock, Alfred	Grant, Cary
North by Northwest	Hitchcock, Alfred	Saint, Eva Marie
Rope	Hitchcock, Alfred	Stewart, James
Psycho	Hitchcock, Alfred	Perkins, Anthony
Psycho	Hitchcock, Alfred	Leigh, Janet
The Birds	Hitchcock, Alfred	Taylor, Rod
The Birds	Hitchcock, Alfred	Hedren, Tippi
Vertigo	Hitchcock, Alfred	Stewart, James
Vertigo	Hitchcock, Alfred	Novak, Kim
Rear Window	Hitchcock, Alfred	Stewart, James
Rear Window	Hitchcock, Alfred	Kelly, Grace
Samson and Delilah	De Mille, Cecil B.	Mature, Victor
The Ten Commandments	De Mille, Cecil B.	Heston, Charlton
Guess Who's Coming to Dinner	Kramer, Stanley	Tracy, Spencer
Guess Who's Coming to Dinner	Kramer, Stanley	Hepburn, Katherine
Judgment at Nuremburg	Kramer, Stanley	Tracy, Spencer
Dr. Strangelove	Kubrick, Stanley	Sellers, Peter
Dr. Strangelove	Kubrick, Stanley	Scott, George C.
Clockwork Orange	Kubrick, Stanley	McDowell, Malcolm
2001	Kubrick, Stanley	Dullea, Keir
2001	Kubrick, Stanley	Dullea, Keir
The Man with the Golden Arm	Preminger, Otto	Novak, Kim
The Man with the Golden Arm	Preminger, Otto	Sinatra, Frank
Anatomy of a Murder	Preminger, Otto	Stewart, James
Inherit the Wind	Preminger, Otto	Tracy, Spencer
Inherit the Wind	Preminger, Otto	March, Fredric
Laura	Preminger, Otto	Andrews, Dana
The Moon is Blue	Preminger, Otto	McNamara, Maggie
The Moon is Blue	Preminger, Otto	Niven, David
Stagecoach	Ford, John	Wayne, John

Mogambo	Ford, John	Gable, Clark
Mogambo	Ford, John	Kelly, Grace
Grapes of Wrath	Ford, John	Fonda, Henry

41. 1, 1 - 2, 2 - 7, 7 - 11, 10 - 12, 11 -15, 13 - 23, 20.
43. 10, Guess Who's Coming to Dinner - 13, Judgment at Nuremberg.

CHAPTER 2

1.

```
CREATE TABLE DIRECTOR
    (DIRNUMB        DECIMAL(3)        NOT NULL,
     DIRNAME        CHAR(18)          NOT NULL,
     DIRBORN        DECIMAL(4)        NOT NULL,
     DIRDIED        DECIMAL(4) )

CREATE TABLE STAR
    (STARNUMB       DECIMAL(4)        NOT NULL,
     STARNAME       CHAR(18)          NOT NULL,
     BRTHPLCE       CHAR(25),
     STARBORN       DECIMAL(4)        NOT NULL,
     STARDIED       DECIMAL(4) )

CREATE TABLE MOVIE
    (MVNUMB         DECIMAL(4)        NOT NULL,
     MVTITLE        CHAR(30)          NOT NULL,
     YRMDE          DECIMAL(4)        NOT NULL,
     MVTYPE         CHAR(6),
     CRIT           DECIMAL(1),
     MPAA           CHAR(2),
     NOMS           DECIMAL(1),
     AWRD           DECIMAL(1),
     DIRNUMB        DECIMAL(3) )

CREATE TABLE MOVSTAR
    (MVNUMB         DECIMAL(4)        NOT NULL,
     STARNUMB       DECIMAL(4)        NOT NULL)

CREATE TABLE MEMBER
    (MMBNUMB        DECIMAL(4)        NOT NULL,
     MMBNAME        CHAR(16)          NOT NULL,
     MMBADDR        CHAR(12)          NOT NULL,
     MMBCTY         CHAR(10)          NOT NULL,
     MMBST          CHAR(2)           NOT NULL,
     NUMRENT        DECIMAL(3)        NOT NULL,
     BONUS          DECIMAL(2)        NOT NULL,
     JOINDATE       DATE              NOT NULL)
```

```
CREATE TABLE TAPE
    (TPNUMB      DECIMAL(4)       NOT NULL,
     MVNUMB      DECIMAL(4)       NOT NULL,
     PURDATE     DATE             NOT NULL,
     TMSRNT      DECIMAL(3)       NOT NULL,
     MMBNUMB     DECIMAL(4) )
```

CHAPTER 3

Use SQL to do the following:

1.

```
SELECT MMBNUMB, MMBNAME, MMBADDR
    FROM MEMBER
```

3.

```
SELECT *
    FROM DIRECTOR
```

5.

```
SELECT TPNUMB
    FROM TAPE
    WHERE TMSRENT >= 10
```

7.

```
SELECT MVNUMB, MVTITLE
    FROM MOVIE
    WHERE MPAA = 'PG'
```

9.

```
SELECT MVNUMB, MVTITLE
    FROM MOVIE
    WHERE MPAA = 'PG'
    OR AWRD >= 1
```

11.

```
SELECT MMBNUMB, MMBNAME
    FROM MEMBER
    WHERE NUMRENT > 10
    AND NUMRENT < 20
```

or

```
SELECT MMBNUMB, MMBNAME
      FROM MEMBER
      WHERE NUMRENT BETWEEN 10 AND 20
```

13.

```
SELECT DIRNUMB, DIRNAME, (DIRDIED - DIRBORN)
      FROM DIRECTOR
      WHERE DIRDIED IS NOT NULL
```

15.

```
SELECT MVNUMB, MVTITLE
      FROM MOVIE
      WHERE MVTYPE IN ('COMEDY', 'RELIGI', 'SUSPEN')
```

17.

```
SELECT MMBNUMB, MMBNAME, MMBADDR, MMBCTY, MMBST, JOINDATE
      FROM MEMBER
      ORDER BY MMBST, MMBCTY
```

19.

```
SELECT COUNT(*)
      FROM MOVIE
      WHERE MVTYPE = 'SUSPEN'
```

21.

```
SELECT COUNT (DISTINCT MMBNUMB)
      FROM TAPE
```

23.

```
SELECT MMBNUMB, MMBNAME
      FROM MEMBER
      WHERE NUMRENT >
            (SELECT AVG(NUMRENT)
                  FROM MEMBER)
```

25.

```
SELECT DIRNUMB, SUM(AWRD)
    FROM MOVIE
    GROUP BY DIRNUMB
    HAVING SUM(AWRD) >= 4
```

27.

```
SELECT DIRNUMB, SUM(AWRD)
    FROM MOVIE
    WHERE MVTYPE = 'COMEDY'
    GROUP BY DIRNUMB
    HAVING SUM(AWRD) >= 1
```

CHAPTER 4

Use SQL to do the following:

1.

```
SELECT MVNUMB, MVTITLE, MOVIE.DIRNUMB, DIRNAME
    FROM MOVIE, DIRECTOR
    WHERE MOVIE.DIRNUMB = DIRECTOR.DIRNUMB
```

3.

```
SELECT MVNUMB, MVTITLE, MOVIE.DIRNUMB, DIRNAME
    FROM MOVIE, DIRECTOR
    WHERE MOVIE.DIRNUMB = DIRECTOR.DIRNUMB
    AND MVTYPE = 'COMEDY'
```

5.

```
SELECT TPNUMB, MVNUMB, TAPE.MMBNUMB, MMBNAME
    FROM TAPE, MEMBER
    WHERE TAPE.MMBNUMB = MEMBER.MMBNUMB
```

7.

```
SELECT DIRNUMB, DIRNAME
    FROM DIRECTOR
    WHERE DIRNUMB NOT IN
            (SELECT DIRNUMB
                FROM MOVIE
                WHERE MVTYPE = 'COMEDY')
```

9.

```
SELECT STAR.STARNUMB, STARNAME
    FROM STAR, MOVIE, MOVSTAR
    WHERE STAR.STARNUMB = MOVSTAR.STARNUMB
    AND MOVIE.MVNUMB = MOVSTAR.MVNUMB
    AND MVTYPE = 'COMEDY'
```

or

```
SELECT STARNUMB, STARNAME
    FROM STAR
    WHERE STARNUMB IN
            (SELECT STARNUMB
                FROM MOVSTAR, MOVIE
                WHERE MOVSTAR.MVNUMB = MOVIE.MVNUMB
                AND MVTYPE = 'COMEDY')
```

11.

```
SELECT F.MVNUMB, F.MVTITLE, S.MVNUMB, S.MVTITLE
    FROM MOVIE F, MOVIE S
    WHERE F.MVTYPE = S.MVTYPE
    AND F.DIRNUMB = S.DIRNUMB
    AND F.MVNUMB < S.MVNUMB
```

13.

```
SELECT TPNUMB, TAPE.MVNUMB
    FROM MOVIE, TAPE, MEMBER
    WHERE MOVIE.MVNUMB = TAPE.MVNUMB
    AND MVTYPE = 'COMEDY'
    AND TAPE.MMBNUMB = MEMBER.MMBNUMB
    AND MMBNAME = 'Peterson, Mark'
```

or

```
SELECT TPNUMB, TAPE.MVNUMB
    FROM MOVIE, TAPE
    WHERE MOVIE.MVNUMB = TAPE.MVNUMB
    AND MVTYPE = 'COMEDY'
    AND MMBNUMB IN
            (SELECT MMBNUMB
                FROM MEMBER
                WHERE MMBNAME = 'Peterson, Mark')
```

15.

```
SELECT TPNUMB, TAPE.MVNUMB
    FROM MOVIE, TAPE
    WHERE MOVIE.MVNUMB = TAPE.MVNUMB
    AND MVTYPE = 'COMEDY'
    AND MMBNUMB NOT IN
        (SELECT MMBNUMB
            FROM MEMBER
            WHERE MMBNAME = 'Peterson, Mark')
```

17. The answer to the previous exercise is:

```
SELECT MVNUMB, MVTITLE
    FROM MOVIE
    WHERE AWRD > ALL
        (SELECT AWRD
            FROM MOVIE, DIRECTOR
            WHERE MOVIE.DIRNUMB = DIRECTOR.DIRNUMB
            AND DIRNAME = 'Allen, Woody')
```

so the answer to this exercise is:

```
SELECT MVNUMB, MVTITLE
    FROM MOVIE
    WHERE AWRD > ALL
        (SELECT AWRD
            FROM MOVIE, DIRECTOR
            WHERE MOVIE.DIRNUMB = DIRECTOR.DIRNUMB
            AND DIRNAME = 'Ford, John')
```

which lists the movie number and title of all movies that won more awards than at least one movie directed by Woody Allen.

CHAPTER 5

Use SQL to make the following changes to the Movies database. After each change, execute an appropriate query to determine whether the correct change was made.

1.

```
UPDATE MEMBER
    SET MMBADDR = '801 College'
    WHERE MMBNUMB = 4
```

3.

```
INSERT INTO TAPE (TPNUMB, MVNUMB, PURDATE, TMSRENT)
    VALUES
    (28, 20, 4/01/91, 0)
```

5.

```
DELETE FROM TAPE
    WHERE MMBNUMB = 2
DELETE FROM MEMBER
    WHERE MMBNUMB = 2
```

7.

```
UPDATE TAPE
    SET MMBNUMB = NULL
    WHERE TPNUMB = 4
```

9.

```
ALTER TABLE MEMBER
    DELETE BONUS
```

11.

```
DROP TABLE TAPE
```

CHAPTER 6

1. a.

```
CREATE VIEW SMALLMMB AS
    SELECT MMBNUMB, MMBNAME, MMBADDR, MMBCTY, MMBST,
            NUMRENT, BONUS
        FROM MEMBER
        WHERE NUMRENT < 20
```

   b.

```
SELECT MMBNUMB, MMBNAME
    FROM SMALLMMB
    WHERE BONUS > 0
```

c.

```
SELECT MMBNUMB, MMBNAME
      FROM MEMBER
      WHERE BONUS > 0
      AND NUMRENT < 20
```

d. The missing column (JOINDATE) must accept nulls since it cannot be entered through this view. Other than that, there are no problems.

3. a.

```
CREATE VIEW RNTNUM (TMSRENT, NUMTAPES) AS
      SELECT TMSRENT, COUNT(*)
            FROM TAPES
            GROUP BY TMSRENT
```

b.

```
SELECT TMSRENT, NUMTAPES
      FROM RNTNUM
      WHERE NUMTAPES > 3
```

c.

```
SELECT TMSRENT, COUNT(*)
      FROM TAPES
      GROUP BY TMSRENT
      HAVING COUNT(*) > 3
```

d. Since this view involves statistics, it is not possible to update the database through this view.

5.

```
REVOKE SELECT ON MEMBER TO SANDERS
```

7.

```
DROP INDEX MOVIND3
```

9.

```
CREATE TABLE MOVIE
    (MMBNUMB      DECIMAL(4)      NOT NULL,
     MVTITLE      CHAR(30)        NOT NULL,
     YRMADE       DECIMAL(4)      NOT NULL,
```

```
        MVTYPE      CHAR(6),
        CRIT        DECIMAL(1),
        MPAA        CHAR(2),
        NOMS        DECIMAL(1),
        AWRD        DECIMAL(1),
        DIRNUMB     DECIMAL(3)
        CHECK (MOVIE.MVTYPE IN ('COMEDY','SUSPEN','RELIGI',
                    'SCI FI','HORROR','DRAMA'))
        PRIMARY KEY (MVNUMB)
        FOREIGN KEY (DIRNUMB) REFERENCES DIRECTOR)
```

CHAPTER 7

1. a.

```
EXEC SQL
    SELECT STARNAME, BRTHPLCE
        INTO :W-STARNAME, :W-BRTHPLCE
        FROM STAR
        WHERE STARNUMB = :W-STARNUMB
END-EXEC
```

b.

```
EXEC SQL
SELECT MVTITLE, MVTYPE, DIRECTOR.DIRNUMB, DIRNAME
    INTO :W-MVTITLE, :W-MVTYPE, :W-DIRNUMB, :W-DIRNAME
    FROM DIRECTOR, MOVIE
    WHERE MVNUMB = :W-MVNUMB
    AND DIRECTOR.DIRNUMB = MOVIE.DIRNUMB
END-EXEC
```

c.

```
DISPLAY 'MEMBER NUMBER: '.
ACCEPT W-MMBNUMB.
DISPLAY 'MEMBER NAME: '.
ACCEPT W-MMBNAME.
    .
    .
    .
EXEC SQL
    INSERT
        INTO MEMBER
        VALUES (:W-MMBNUMB, :W-MMBNAME, :W-MMBADDR,
            :W-MMBCTY, :W-MMBST, :W-NUMBRENT, :W-BONUS)
END-EXEC
```

d.

```
EXEC SQL
    UPDATE MEMBER
        SET MMBNAME = :W-MMBNAME
        WHERE MMBNUMB = :W-MMBNUMB
END-EXEC
```

e.

```
EXEC SQL
    UPDATE MEMBER
        SET BONUS = BONUS + :W-ADDITIONAL-BONUS
        WHERE MMBNUMB = :W-MMBNUMB
END-EXEC
```

f.

```
EXEC SQL
    DELETE
        FROM TAPE
        WHERE TPNUMB = :W-TPNUMB
END-EXEC
```

CHAPTER 8

1. COMMIT makes all the updates since the last COMMIT permanent. It also makes them available to other users. ROLLBACK reverses all the updates since the last commit.

3.

```
CREATE DOMAIN MVTYPES CHAR(6)
    CHECK (VALUE = 'COMEDY' OR VALUE = 'DRAMA' OR
    VALUE = 'HORROR' OR VALUE = 'RELIGI' OR
    VALUE = 'SUSPEN' OR VALUE = 'WESTER' )

CREATE TABLE MOVIE
    (MVNUMB       DECIMAL(4),
    MVTITLE       CHAR(30),
    YRMADE        DECIMAL(4),
    MVTYPE        MVTYPES,
    CRIT          DECIMAL(1),
    MPAA          CHAR(2),
    NOMS          DECIMAL(1),
    AWRD          DECIMAL(1),
    DIRNUMB       DECIMAL(3))
```

5.

```
SELECT TPNUMB, MVNUMB
      FROM MOVIE
      WHERE MVTYPE = 'COMEDY'
INTERSECT
SELECT MEMBER.TPNUMB, MVNUMB
      FROM MEMBER, TAPE
      WHERE MEMBER.TPNUMB = TAPE.TPNUMB
      AND MMBNAME = 'Peterson, Mark'
```

7.

```
CREATE ASSERTION A1 CHECK
      ( NOT EXISTS (SELECT STARNUMB, COUNT(*)
                        FROM MOVSTAR
                        GROUP BY STARNUMB
                        HAVING COUNT(*) > 8)
```

9. SQLCODE was not totally standardized. Different vendors assigned different meanings to the same value. The values of SQLSTATE, on the other hand, are specified as part of the standard.

DISCARD